Oxford Primary Social Studies

My Country and Me

4

Pat Lunt

Oxford University Press

Contents

Unit 1 Culture and identity — 3

1.1	Knowing myself	4
1.2	Values and society	6
1.3	Role models	8
1.4	Families and values	10
1.5	Being independent	12
1.6	National symbols	14
1.7	National celebrations	16
1.8	Customs and culture	18
1.9	Clothing and culture	20
1.10	Culture and faith	22
	Review questions	24

Unit 2 History and heritage — 25

2.1	The region's ancient history	26
2.2	Early civilisations	28
2.3	Worldwide trade begins	30
2.4	Ancient worldwide trade	32
2.5	The arrival of Islam	34
	Review questions	36

Unit 3 People and places — 37

3.1	Using maps 1	38
3.2	Using maps 2	40
3.3	Coordinates	42
3.4	Latitude and longitude	44
3.5	Rainfall charts	46
3.6	Temperature and wind charts	48
3.7	Water resources	50
3.8	Renewable or non-renewable?	52
3.9	Oil, gas and minerals	54
3.10	Resources from the sea	56
3.11	Population	58
3.12	People and places	60
	Review questions	62

Unit 4 Citizenship — 63

4.1	Social groups and society	64
4.2	Behaviour in society	66
4.3	Human rights	68
4.4	Children's rights	70
4.5	The local environment	72
4.6	Practical local action	74
4.7	Personal communications	76
4.8	Mass media	78
4.9	Public information	80
4.10	Advertising	82
4.11	Government	84
4.12	Laws	86
4.13	The economy 1	88
4.14	The economy 2	90
4.15	Service industries	92
4.16	Work	94
4.17	Household spending	96
4.18	Money matters	98
	Review questions	100

Unit 5 Health and wellbeing — 101

5.1	Good food 1	102
5.2	Good food 2	104
5.3	Respiration and circulation	106
5.4	Happiness	108
5.5	What makes people happy?	110
5.6	Rest and relaxation	112
5.7	Be safe on the internet 1	114
5.8	Be safe on the internet 2	116
	Review questions	118

Glossary — 119

1 Culture and identity

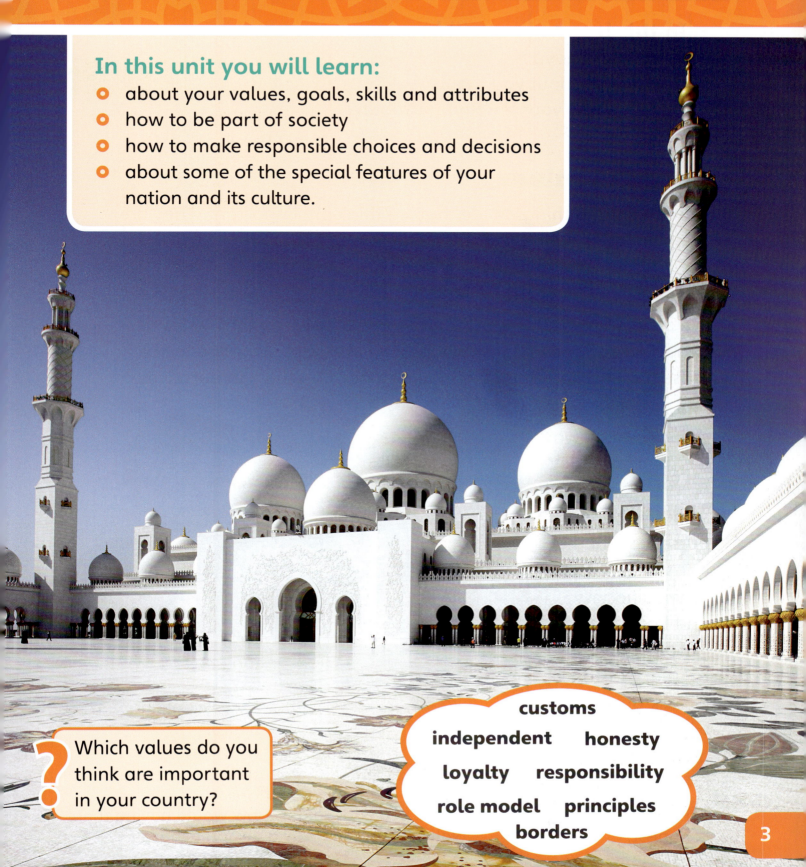

In this unit you will learn:
- about your values, goals, skills and attributes
- how to be part of society
- how to make responsible choices and decisions
- about some of the special features of your nation and its culture.

? Which values do you think are important in your country?

customs
independent   honesty
loyalty   responsibility
role model   principles
borders

1.1 Knowing myself

In this lesson you will learn:
- to consider your personal values
- to think about your goals
- to identify your skills and attributes.

Personal values

Values are the things in life that we think are important. They are the **principles** we try to follow. Our values help to make us who we are. Values determine the way we relate to other people and to the world around us.

We develop values as we start to appreciate certain attitudes or behaviour such as kindness, honesty and respect. We hope to see these qualities in other people and to develop them in ourselves.

These values can determine the way we speak and act. Before we say or do something we ask ourselves whether it fits with our values. When kindness and honesty are important values to us, for instance, we ask ourselves whether what we are about to say is kind or if what we are about to do is honest.

▲ Some personal values. How would having these values affect the way a person behaves?

Goals and values

Values can help people identify personal goals and how these will be achieved.

Personal goals change as people grow. Very young children are busy learning new skills. They learn to become more independent, thinking and doing more for themselves.

Older children try new hobbies and activities. They find what they enjoy and what interests them. This helps them as they start to think about what they might like to do in the future and what their goals will be.

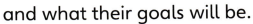

▲ Trying out new activities lets you find out if you enjoy them.

Skills and attributes

We can have skills and attributes to do with a particular subject or activity. Some important skills and attributes, for example concentration and perseverance, can help us when we are learning something new. We also need some special skills and attributes when we are relating to others, for example communication skills, understanding and patience.

We sometimes face times that are challenging and we may need other attributes such as courage and resilience.

Activities

1. Make a list showing goals you have in school now, goals outside school and goals for the future.
2. Write about times when you have had to persevere.

1.2 Values and society

In this lesson you will learn:
- how personal values become shared values
- about shared values in countries of the Arabian Gulf
- how your actions can affect other people.

Shared values

Our values often come from what we think is right or wrong. We call this a sense of morality. When people living together in a **society** agree about what is right or wrong they often share a set of values. These shared values are an important part of the success of the society. The society will also teach its members about those values. This happens within the informal environment of the family and also more formally through the school system and other **institutions**. In this way the values become part of the society's identity. People in the community are expected to behave in ways that reflect the values of society.

Shared values in countries of the Arabian Gulf

Societies in the Arabian Gulf are built on centuries of **traditions** which come from cultural, religious and tribal **heritage**. These traditions have been passed down from one generation to the next and they are the foundations of society. For this reason they should be acknowledged and respected by everyone.

Loyalty is highly valued in Arabian Gulf societies. This means that people are expected to commit to the groups to which they belong, for example by agreeing to follow its rules and demonstrating a sense of responsibility towards one another.

Other values that have been passed down through generations are hospitality and generosity. These values are part of the traditions from the **nomadic** peoples. They were used to living in the harsh conditions of the desert and were always aware that people living in or passing through those places might need food or rest.

Valuing other people

Living in a society means being part of a group. Each person in a group has to be aware of other members and the needs and desires they have. This means that a person's actions have to reflect that awareness. It is not good to behave in a way that prevents other people's needs being met or that causes anyone to be upset or offended.

People who are able to live and behave in a way that matches the values of a society are able to respect themselves and to be respected by others. This requires people to take responsibility for themselves and for their own actions.

▲ Showing hospitality and generosity are important values in Arab societies.

Activities

1. Write about some of the values you think are important in the society in which you live and how they affect the way people live.

2. Work in a group to discuss people's needs in the classroom. Describe the sort of class behaviour that will make sure those needs are met.

1.3 Role models

In this lesson you will learn:
- how a person can be a role model
- to identify role models from different parts of life
- to understand and describe what makes a person a good role model.

Role models

A role model is a person who is admired by other people. People may wish to imitate a role model's general behaviour or wish to achieve a similar degree of success.

Some role models are people who have become well-known because of special achievements in a particular area of life. Other role models are those people whose behaviour sets a good example in everyday situations.

Role models can be from anywhere in the world and also in our family, school and local community.

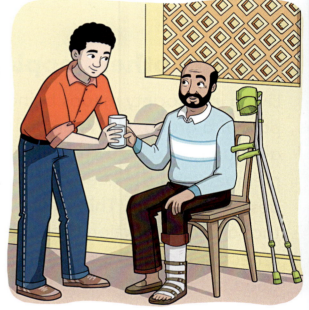

▲ When people show care and kindness they are acting as a good role model for others in society.

Role models in school

Good role models in school are those members of the school community who do all that they can to make sure that everybody's experience of being in the school is as good as it can be. These students behave in a way that the school expects.

That means that they follow school and class rules and work hard in their studies. It also means that they care about other people's feelings and rights. They care about the school and its values. They want to use some of their time and skills to make the school as good as it can be for everyone.

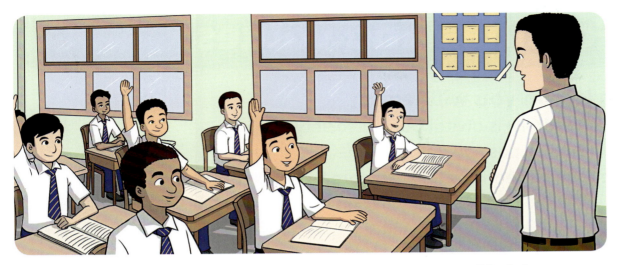

▲ Taking part in class discussions is an important way of helping learning to take place in school.

There may also be certain students in school who achieve success in a particular part of a school's life, for example by reaching a certain level of achievement in a certain subject, by representing the school in a particular activity or by being active in promoting an aspect of school life such as environmental awareness. These individuals can be role models for others who want to achieve similar things.

Role models in society

In the wider world we also hear about people who are held up as examples for others to follow. These can be people who achieve success in sport, devote themselves to working for charity or overcome serious difficulties and challenges.

▲ Sportspeople such as Mohammed Al Hammadi encourage people to do their best whatever their circumstances.

Activities

1. Work in a group and prepare a list of qualities, behaviours and attitudes you think a good role model in school would have.
2. Carry out some research into a person you think is a good role model.

1.4 Families and values

In this lesson you will learn:
- that the family is a vital part of society
- how families pass on values
- what people learn as they prepare to enter society.

The family unit

A family unit is made up of parents and children, together with other people who are related, including grandparents, uncles, aunts and cousins. Relationships are very close within a family unit and children can learn many important lessons from parents and elders.

People feel a strong sense of belonging to the family unit. This sense remains strong even when the number of relationships increases as families join together through marriage or when families relate to each other as part of a wider community.

Passing on values

In families, values are passed on from one generation to another. Children witness the actions, speech and behaviour of other family members and they assume that this is the correct way to behave. They follow the example of their parents and relatives. Some values, however, may need to be taught separately because they are not easily understood without being explained. For example, parents may have to teach a child about being honest.

▲ A person who is treated with care and respect is more likely to treat others in the same way.

The family and society

The family provides the environment in which children learn about behaviour that is acceptable or unacceptable in society. Socially acceptable behaviour reflects the values of society. Parents are responsible for telling their children about the traditions and values of the society in which they live.

In countries of the Arabian Gulf, societies are based on the values of Islam and the traditions of Arab culture. As a result, love, kindness, respect and the family are all important principles.

Dealing with change

Change is a part of life. Traditional ideas and values within a culture can be influenced by new ideas and values from other cultures. Advances in **technology** also bring about changes to the way people live their lives.

▲ Technology is an important part of many people's lives.

Activities

1 Write about values that are important in your family.
2 Work in a group to prepare some questions to ask your parents about:
   - values that they were taught as children
   - things they think are different about family life today.

1.5 Being independent

In this lesson you will learn:
- to identify the benefits of being in a family
- to identify ways in which children become independent
- to describe how family members depend on each other.

Benefits of being in a family

Babies are born helpless. They survive because of the care they receive from their family.

Children gain more knowledge and learn new skills as they grow, including how to live with other people.

As we spend so much time with other people we must learn to be aware of their needs instead of just our own. Being in a family helps us learn how to do this.

▲ Learning manners is a part of understanding how to live with other people.

Sharing life in a family

Family members have different roles. Parents provide for the physical and emotional needs of family members and teach children how to live in their society. Children learn to show love and respect and to help in practical ways.

◀ Every family member can help in different ways.

Becoming independent

Children become more independent as they grow. They can do more things for themselves and rely less on other people. They can make more choices and decisions for themselves. This means they also have responsibility for what happens as a result of those choices and decisions.

Being independent does not mean we do not think about others. Our choices and decisions often affect other people. We must learn to compromise and to make choices and decisions that take other people into account. Learning to do this in a family helps because we are with people who love us and care for us even if we do not always agree.

◀ Whose responsibility is it to make sure that you have everything you need for school?

Activities

1 Make a list of the things your family provides for you and teaches you.

2 Work in a group to discuss:
- the areas where you have certain choices
- how decisions are made in your family.

1 Culture and identity

1.6 National symbols

In this lesson you will learn:
- to identify and describe symbols associated with your country.

A national symbol is something that is used to represent a country to all the people living in that country and also to the rest of the world. The symbol encourages a sense of belonging, identity and loyalty. It also helps the people of a country to feel proud of their nation. Since national symbols have this role it is important to treat them with respect.

A national symbol represents things about a country such as its history, its values and its people.

Flags

National flags are used to represent a country and are flown from masts on government buildings, on schools and in other public places. Almost all the national flags of the world are rectangular and they have at least two separate colours. The colours are often shown in horizontal or vertical bands. Colours are chosen to represent something special about the country, its history or its rulers.

▲ National flags flying outside the United Nations headquarters.

Did you know?

Ships are registered to a particular country and they fly a special version of that country's flag when they are at sea.

Emblems

A national emblem is a symbol which is designed to represent important parts of a nation. The emblem will sometimes show animals that are found in the country. Sometimes the animals are used to represent something else, such as bravery or wisdom. A national emblem will often have the colours of the national flag somewhere in the design. There may also be writing which can be the name of the country or a special **motto**.

Other symbols

Certain birds, flowers and trees can be a special part of a country and so they become symbols of that country. They are also often shown within other symbols such as the national emblem. If there is a special history of a particular trade such as fishing or seafaring, this can also appear as a symbol of a country.

▲ A falcon can be seen in the emblem of many countries of the Arabian Gulf.

National anthems

A national anthem is a special song which is used by a country to express feelings of national identity and pride. National anthems are often sung at special occasions and also daily in schools as an expression of loyalty to a nation and its rulers.

Activity

Work in a group to prepare an illustrated presentation about the national flag and emblems of a country in the Arabian Gulf.

1.7 National celebrations

In this lesson you will learn:
- to identify and describe national celebrations in your country.

National celebrations are held to mark or remember important events in a country. There may also be holidays and festivals to mark important religious events and special times.

National celebrations remembering history

The history of the people of the Arabian Peninsula goes back many thousands of years but the countries that we know today are not all that old. The **borders** of the modern countries were not established because certain territory was understood to be under the control of a particular tribal leader. In some areas, the way people lived was also partly controlled by people from other countries and they were not completely free to govern themselves. When they became free to do this they became **independent**.

The date when a country was founded or when it became independent is very important for a country and its people. In many countries of the Arabian Gulf the date is marked by a national celebration, often called National Day. Other National Day celebrations mark the anniversary of the day when the ruler came to power.

National celebrations from religion

Religions have celebrations when special events are remembered. When a religion forms an important part of the culture of a country then there are national celebrations to mark those religious events. Islam is the national religion of societies in the Arabian Gulf so here there are a number of celebrations to mark significant events from Islam's history.

The major celebrations are *Eid-al-Fitr*, held at the end of Ramadan, and *Eid-ul-Adha*, which is the feast of sacrifice.

In *Eid-al-Fitr* people are celebrating the end of fasting but also giving thanks that they have been given the strength by Allah to exercise the required self-control for the month of Ramadan.

In *Eid-al-Adha* people celebrate Ibrahim's complete obedience to Allah and remind themselves of their own submission and desire to obey. Both celebrations involve feasting, special prayers and sometimes the exchange of cards or gifts.

▲ *Iftar* is the special meal taken during Ramadan from sunset onwards after a day of fasting.

Features of national celebrations

National celebrations are special occasions. There are many ways in which people recognise this special time when people get together with family and friends. They might wear their best clothes or even have special clothes for the occasion. People will usually have special food too. Sometimes there are public events which many thousands of people can attend, such as parades and displays of fireworks.

▲ Parades are often a part of National Day celebrations.

Activity

Working in a group, find out about the national celebrations held in the countries of the Arabian Gulf. Find out why they are celebrated and how people mark the different occasions.

1.8 Customs and culture

In this lesson you will learn:
- to identify common values in your country
- that Islamic values are important in Arab countries.

Culture

A culture is a way of life based on a set of ideas, beliefs and values. Parts of a culture can be expressed through art, music and clothing. Other parts of a culture are expressed through certain types of behaviour or actions. Some of these special ways of behaving become known as **customs**.

Customs in countries of the Arabian Gulf

Customs in countries of the Arabian Gulf express the values of Islam and traditional Arab cultures. People are expected to be modest, especially in the way they dress. They should be polite and show respect, especially for their elders. An important part of showing respect starts when people meet and greet one another.

There are a number of common actions when people meet. When men meet they may shake hands, hug, or offer one another a kiss on each cheek. In Arabian Gulf countries men may also briefly touch noses. When women meet for the first time they may also shake hands. Women who know each other may kiss on both cheeks and the number of kisses is a sign of how well the two know one another.

◀ A handshake is a common form of greeting.

Hospitality and generosity are important values. The customs connected to these values are welcoming guests into the home and offering good things to eat and drink. If a guest in a home admires a particular object then the host is quite likely to offer the item as a gift or to offer something of similar value. The guest would cause offence if this offer was refused. The guest would be expected to offer a gift of similar or greater value back to the host.

Respect is another important value which can be seen in many of the specific types of behaviour which are customs, learnt as a part of a culture. For example, in Arab culture, guests are normally expected to show respect by removing their footwear when entering the hosts' rooms within a home.

Arab culture also teaches that respect should especially be shown towards women and elders.

▲ It is polite to hold doors open for other people, especially women.

Activity

Find out about some common customs of your country and one other country. Explain the ideas, beliefs and values that the customs show.

1.9 Clothing and culture

In this lesson you will learn:
- to identify the traditional dress in your country
- to understand that traditional dress is a part of national culture.

Clothing

The Islamic values of modesty and simplicity are reflected in the traditional clothing worn by men and women in societies of the countries of the Arabian Gulf. The clothing also reflects the traditional Arab cultures of the region and is very suitable for the hot, dry climate.

There are sometimes variations within a country that show which region or group a person is from.

Clothing for men

Traditional clothing for men is based around a simple full-length robe that reaches to the ankle. This is usually white in summer to reflect the heat. It can be made from different materials to suit different times of year. Other layers of clothing include outer cloaks and coats which are important in colder areas. In a number of countries the traditional headgear is a chequered headscarf, sometimes called a *ghutrah*. This is worn over the head and is kept in place by a band of coiled rope, traditionally made from camel hair and called an *iqal* or *agal*.

In Oman there are two main types of traditional headgear. The *kuma* is an **embroidered** cap, and the *massar* is an embroidered wool turban.

A wrap or a pair of loose trousers is worn beneath the *dishdasha* to protect and cover the lower body.

On their feet men wear open shoes or sandals.

Clothing for women

Traditional clothing for women includes a long robe or dress, which reaches to the knee or the ankles. The neckline traces around the base of the neck. This and the loose sleeves can be decorated and there is often a tassel hanging from the neckline. Over the dress women wear a long cloak that covers all the body except the face, feet and hands. A woman may also wear a scarf to cover the hair and neck which can be pulled across the face. Some may wear a separate veil to cover the face.

Loose trousers are worn beneath the robe to provide a covering for the legs and ankles. The trousers may be decorated on the ankles. Women may wear certain types of jewellery such as bracelets and necklaces.

Modern influences

Many people today wear western style clothing at least some of the time, although traditional clothing is more comfortable in the climate.

▲ Jewellery has been important in the region of the Arabian Gulf for centuries and the craftsmen of the past were very skilful.

▲ People are expected to show respect for the culture and tradition of showing modesty in clothing.

Activities

1. Work in a group to find out about the traditional dress for a man or a woman in the country in which you are living. Make a labelled drawing.

2. Make a labelled drawing of traditional dress for a boy or girl in your country and one other country.

1.10 Culture and faith

In this lesson you will learn:
- to identify ways in which Islam influences daily life and culture
- to recognise the attitude of rulers and governments to other faith traditions.

When people from different cultural backgrounds create a society together this is known as a multicultural society. As faith is often an important part of culture a multicultural society will probably include people from different faiths.

The faith of countries in the Arabian Gulf is Islam and this guides all parts of life.

Daily life

Daily life revolves around the requirement for all Muslims to pray. Prayer is one of the five pillars of Islam and so is extremely important. Prayer takes place at five set times during the day:

- *Fajr*: from first light to sunrise
- *Dhuhr* or *Zuhr*: at midday, after the sun has passed its highest point
- *Asr*: later in the afternoon
- *Maghrib*: just after the sun goes down, at sunset
- *Isha*: in the evening, after complete darkness has fallen.

This daily cycle of prayers sets the pattern for daily life.

Friday is the most holy day of the week and the weekend is Friday and Saturday. Some businesses and shops close during Friday prayers.

Special festivals

Ramadan is the holiest month in the Islamic calendar when Muslims fast during the day between sunrise and sunset as one of the five pillars of Islam.

Since Muslims are fasting during the day at this time, it is respectful for non-Muslims to avoid eating and drinking in public. During Ramadan, Muslims break their daily fast at the end of the day with a special meal called *Iftar*.

Festivals such as *Eid-ul-Fitr*, which ends the fast of Ramadan, and *Eid-ul-Adha*, the feast of sacrifice, are public holidays.

▲ Festivals are a time for thankful prayers, family togetherness and celebration.

Other faiths

An important part of Islam is openness, tolerance and respect. The enlightened rulers of many countries of the Arabian Gulf region have stated that non-Muslim people should be free to practise their own faith.

There are many examples where the ruler of a country has granted non-Muslims the right to build places of worship and even donated the land on which they could be built.

Challenges and opportunities

Islam provides the guiding principles for daily life in countries of the Arabian Gulf. These countries also show that people of different cultures and faiths are able to live together peacefully and with respect for one another.

Activities

1 Draw and label a set of pictures that show when Muslims are required to pray throughout a day.

2 Work in a group to make a list of guidelines that will help people to live up to the Islamic values of tolerance and respect.

Unit 1 Review questions

1 If people in a society have the same values it means they:
  a have the same kinds of possessions
  b like to wear similar clothes
  c share ideas about what is truly important in life
  d use public transport

2 A person whose general behaviour is admired and who sets a good example is:
  a an athlete
  b a role model
  c a doctor
  d a charity worker

3 As we become more independent it means:
  a we no longer have to think about other people
  b we are not responsible for what happens when we make choices
  c we have to look after other people
  d we make our own choices and take responsibility for the consequences

4 A country that is completely free to govern itself is said to be:
  a enclosed
  b independent
  c interdependent
  d determined

5 Write about two values that are important to you and say why each one is important.

6 Describe two qualities you admire in people and say why these qualities might make these people good role models.

7 Describe three decisions you are responsible for making at home, at school or in a club or group to which you belong.

8 Write about three of the national symbols of the country in which you are living.

9 Describe the customs of your country that are to do with people's behaviour when they meet.

10 Describe some items of traditional clothing from your country and explain why wearing these might be important to some people.

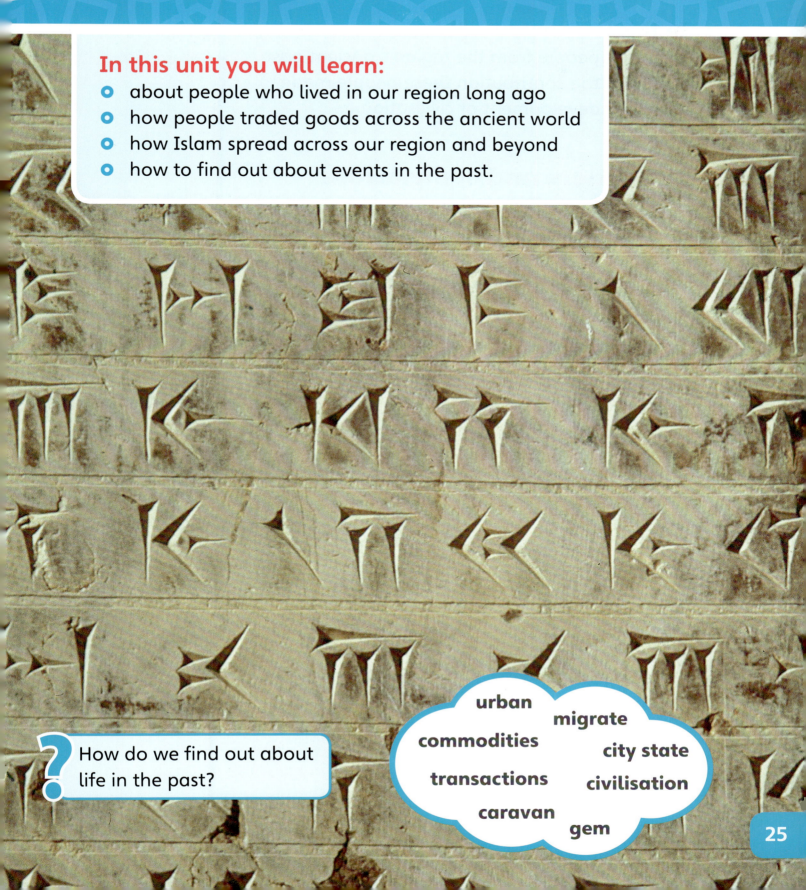

2 History and heritage

In this unit you will learn:
- about people who lived in our region long ago
- how people traded goods across the ancient world
- how Islam spread across our region and beyond
- how to find out about events in the past.

? How do we find out about life in the past?

urban
commodities
transactions
caravan
migrate
city state
civilisation
gem

2.1 The region's ancient history

In this lesson you will learn:
- about people from the region's ancient past
- about the contribution these people made to the development of civilisation.

First settlers and civilisations

Early people lived as hunter-gatherers, collecting food from trees and plants and adding to their diet by hunting wild animals. Later they settled as farmers, planting crops and keeping animals.

One of the earliest settled **civilisations** developed in an area known as Mesopotamia. This fertile area was centred round the systems of two great rivers, the Tigris and the Euphrates, on land now made up of parts of modern-day Kuwait, Iraq and northern Syria.

A people, known as the Sumerians, **migrated** to this area between 3500–3100 **BCE**. They developed the earliest **urban** civilisation in the world, where the people lived in **city states**.

◀ Ancient Mesopotamia, as it was about 5500 years ago, showing important cities.

Power struggles

The people of the different cities fought one another to become the most powerful. The Assyrians from Assur and the people of the city of Babylon held control of the region for hundreds of years. The whole area was taken over in 539 BCE by an army led by a king known as Cyrus the Great.

Contributions to civilisation

Although there were many conflicts this was also a time of creativity and there were many inventions in different parts of life.

Inventions from the Sumerian period include the first writing system, the wheel, ploughs pulled by animals, glazed pottery and paved roads. The Sumerians also developed a system of maths. They combined this with study of the moon, stars and planets and created the first calendar.

However creative people were they still needed resources. The Sumerians had most things but not enough stone, wood and metal. They needed to trade with other parts of the world to get these. For this reason they became skilful shipbuilders.

▲ An ancient mural of Assyrian soldiers.

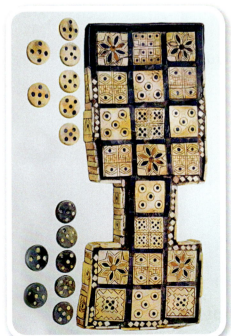

◀ There was obviously time for relaxing in ancient Mesopotamia. This board game, found in modern Iraq, is known as the Royal Game of Ur. It was made between 2600 and 2400 BCE.

Activity

Research and write about some of the inventions of the Sumerians.

2.2 Early civilisations

In this lesson you will learn:
- how trade in the Arabian Gulf developed
- to identify countries that were part of early trading.

Early civilisations and trade

An ancient civilisation, called Dilmun, developed in the eastern part of the Arabian Peninsula. Its location meant that it had an important role in the development and control of trade. The people of Mesopotamia wanted copper, which was mined in what is now Oman. The people of the Arabian Gulf needed food, since they could not produce enough to feed themselves. Mesopotamia had plenty of grain and other foods to spare, as well as wool for clothing so they traded with the Arabian Gulf.

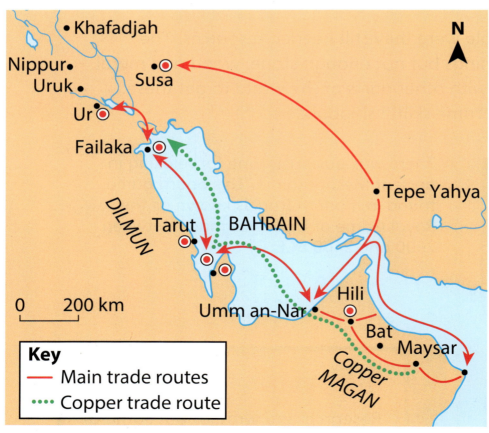

▲ The Arabian Gulf, showing important trade routes that existed four to five thousand years ago.

Pieces of ancient pottery found in many places show that pots were an important part of trade. Precious **gems** called pearls were also traded. These were found in the oysters that lived in the warm waters of the Arabian Gulf.

Other civilisations developed in the area of the Arabian Peninsula that is present-day Yemen (see the map above). People lived in organised kingdoms based on **agriculture** and trade. Frankincense and myrrh also came from here. These two substances became some of the most valuable **commodities** in the world.

▲ The ancient south-eastern kingdoms of the Arabian Peninsula and the main cities

Transportation

Many goods traded through the Dilmun civilisation travelled by boat. Sea routes went around the coast and up the Red Sea. There were also important routes over land from the south, heading northwards across the Arabian Peninsula.

Because of its geographical location, the Arabian Peninsula was at the centre of worldwide trade.

Activities

1. Work in a group to answer the following questions. Use the text to help you.
   - Why did the people in the different areas of the region need to trade?
   - What sort of evidence is there to show that trade happened?
   - What are the two ways in which trade took place?
   - What were two resources traded in the region?
2. Make up a short role play that shows people of the time deciding that they need to trade with people from another country.

2.3 Worldwide trade begins

In this lesson you will learn:
- to identify the goods that were important to early traders
- to understand the importance of the location of the Arabian Gulf for trade
- to identify countries that were part of early worldwide trading.

The beginnings of worldwide trade

Evidence shows that trade took place over very long distances thousands of years ago. Large scale trade developed based on precious goods such as incense, silk and spices. The location of the Arabian Peninsula meant that it always had an important role in this trade.

Incense

Incense is a resin that comes from certain trees. It is burned for its smell or used to add scent to perfumes and oils. It was used for treating or preventing illness and in many ancient religious ceremonies. Frankincense and myrrh are well-known examples of incense and come from the areas of modern-day Yemen and Oman.

A network of trade routes existed by land and sea when the height of trade in frankincense was reached between 200 BCE and 100 **CE**.

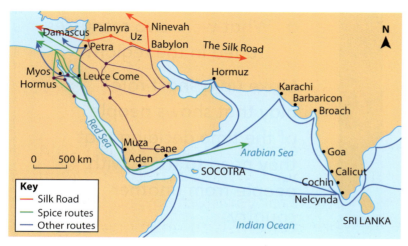

▲ **A** The overland and sea-going routes of the incense trade.

Did you know?

It took 62 days to travel from one end of the Incense Route, in the southern Arabian Peninsula, to the other end on the Mediterranean coast.

Silk

Silk fibres come from the cocoons made by certain moth caterpillars. The silk cloth made from these fibres has always been a luxury. Silk was traded West from China along the Silk Road to the Mediterranean Sea from about 220 BCE to 1450 CE. Incense and other goods were traded East.

▲ Silk is made from the fibres created by silk moth caterpillars.

Spices

Spices include cinnamon, turmeric, pepper and ginger. Many spices come from islands in South-east Asia. Records suggest that trade in spices was taking place with the Middle East and Egypt as long ago as 3000 BCE.

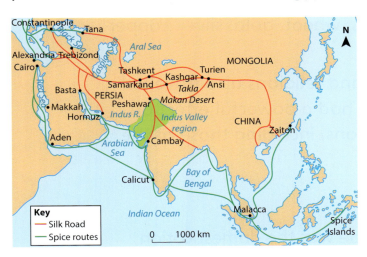

The position of the Arabian Peninsula between the spice-producing areas and the markets of Africa and Europe meant that the spice merchants of the region could control the trade.

◀ B The Silk Road and Spice Trade routes

Activities

1. On a world map, mark the countries involved in the early trade in incense, spices and silk and the main routes taken by traders in these goods.

2. Imagine you are a merchant in ancient times planning to go on a journey along a major trading route. Write a letter to a friend explaining how you have prepared for your journey, how long you think you will be away, what concerns you have and what goods you hope to bring back.

2.4 Ancient worldwide trade

In this lesson you will learn:
- to identify and describe some of the effects of early trade on civilisations
- about the role of the Arabian Peninsula in the development of the ancient world.

The effects of worldwide trade

Ancient trade in incense, spices and silk took place between the continents of Europe and Asia and across many countries. Ancient documents show that other goods were also traded including embroidered cloth, fine linen, animals, wheat, gold, silver, copper and precious stones.

Ideas, inventions, crafts, technology and religions also travelled along these trade routes. All of these had a powerful effect on the development of different civilisations, including those of the Arab World.

Camels

One probable effect of the incense trade was the domestication of the camel for use as pack animals on the routes across the Arabian Peninsula from the southern areas to the ports of the Mediterranean Sea.

Camels were organised into **caravans**, sometimes containing hundreds of animals. This helped to keep costs down. Travelling in a large group also helped to offer protection from bandits.

Shipbuilding

Travelling over land was expensive, partly because it was so slow. A journey along the Silk Road could take over a year. Travel by sea was faster and a single boat could carry much more than several camel caravans.

Trade drove people to build better, bigger and faster ships. Early boats from Mesopotamia were made of reed bundles covered with a special substance to make them waterproof. As ships arrived from other parts of the world local shipbuilders learnt new ideas and how to build ships from wood.

Boats became larger so they could carry more. People invented different kinds of sails and ways of steering the boats. Vessels became even faster and the journeys took less time. Sailors learnt about the types of winds that blew in different places.

Written language

Writing began as pictures which were used to show ideas such as 'brave' and 'strong'. Over time the pictures were used to represent particular sounds. The pictures changed to become special shapes which were quicker and easier to draw. People learnt to recognise what each shape meant. Early writing developed because it was mostly used to record goods kept in storehouses and record **transactions** between traders.

▲ Early writing developed in Mesopotamia is called cuneiform. The shapes were often pressed into tablets of wet clay.

Arts, crafts and technology

Ideas and techniques for use in art, craft and technology were also exchanged along trade routes.

▲ This chalice, dating from 2000–1800 BCE, was found in Bahrain but is thought to have come from the Indus Valley. Look at map B on page 31 and think how the chalice may have travelled to Bahrain.

Activity

Work in a group to make a fact sheet about how ancient trade made people think of new inventions or ways of doing things.

2.5 The arrival of Islam

In this lesson you will learn:
- about the beginnings of Islam
- how Islam spread and influenced the region and the world.

Tribal societies

The societies of ancient times formed around different tribes who were caught in a never-ending round of disputes over land and precious resources. The tribes also had different religious beliefs and practices. Perhaps the most sacred site was the Ka'ba in Makkah which, at that time, was full of the religious idols and images of many different tribes and nations. This was the society into which Islam emerged in 610 CE.

The impact of Islam

The Prophet Muhammad (Peace Be Upon Him) began teaching the people in Makkah but many, influenced by the powerful Quraysh tribe, did not accept his words. The people who did accept them formed a community of believers. This community faced opposition and so they moved to Yathreb (Madinah). This is the migration of the Prophet (Peace Be Upon Him) which is the starting point of the Islamic calendar.

The new faith of Islam acted as a call to Arab peoples to unite as one community which would be based on the ideas of justice in society and a fair sharing of wealth.

The spread of Islam

In the eighth year after his migration, the Prophet (Peace Be Upon Him) returned to Makkah at the head of a large army. The people of Makkah and the surrounding tribes became Muslims and rulers and tribes from all areas of the Arabian Peninsula gradually accepted Islam.

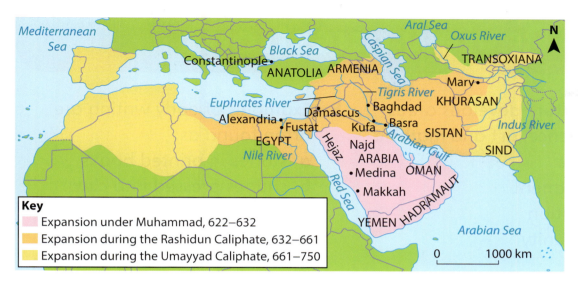

◀ The Muslim Empire by 750 CE.

Islam began to expand beyond the Arabian Peninsula after Muhammad's (Peace Be Upon Him) death. Muhammad (Peace Be Upon Him) had not appointed a leader to follow on from him so the Muslims chose a **caliph** to rule over a **caliphate**.

Muslim territories expanded under the first four caliphs of the Rashidite Caliphate. The Ummayad Caliphate followed and lasted until 750 CE, spreading Islam even further. Across the Muslim empire, coins, weights and measures were all made to have the same values. This, and the spread of Arabic as a common language, made trade much easier.

During the Abbasid Caliphate, which lasted from 750 CE to 1258 CE, there were great achievements in all aspects of life from art and literature to science and mathematics.

▲ Coins from the Ummayad period. Standardised coins, weights and measures made trading much easier.

◀ A stable Islamic empire meant that great advances in all aspects of life could take place. This instrument is called an astrolabe, which was used to help navigate at sea.

Activity

Carry out some research into an achievement made during the period of the caliphates mentioned in the text.

2 History and heritage

Unit 2 Review questions

1. When a culture develops areas such as science, art and maths it is known as:
   a. a department
   b. a civilisation
   c. a community
   d. a city

2. When people move permanently from one area to live in another, this is called:
   a. removing
   b. departing
   c. migrating
   d. arriving

3. People long ago made contact with others in different parts of the world, mainly for:
   a. trade
   b. holidays
   c. sharing ideas
   d. selling artwork

4. The important material that was traded from China was:
   a. wool
   b. nylon
   c. cotton
   d. silk

5. Examples of early writing are often found as:
   a. stories in printed books
   b. shapes pressed into clay tablets
   c. drawings on cave walls
   d. calligraphy on special paper

6. Trade across the early Muslim Empire was made easier by:
   a. trading silk, shoes and wood
   b. taking camels by boat across the Indian Ocean
   c. using the same coins, weights and measures
   d. building large cities

7. Explain why the different resources two groups of people had might lead them to trade with one another.

8. Identify two items that were the basis of early trade across the world and describe how they were transported.

9. Explain how early worldwide trade would have had an impact on shipbuilding or on a craft such as pottery.

10. Explain how the spread of the Arabic language across the early Muslim Empire would have made trade easier.

3 People and places

In this unit you will learn:
- how to use maps and coordinates
- about lines of latitude and longitude
- to understand and draw weather charts
- about some important resources
- why information on population and where people live is useful
- to draw a population chart
- to create informative presentations and posters.

? What is special about using the sun to make electricity?

habitat
non-renewable   capital city
groundwater   sustainability
precipitation
statistics   desalination
terrain   aquifer

3.1 Using maps 1

In these lessons you will learn:
- to identify the different types of information available on maps
- to recognise the different ways in which information is presented on maps.

A map is a special diagram or picture that represents part of the world's surface. We use maps because they give us information about places.

A single map cannot give us all the information we need and so different maps are designed to give particular types of information.

Information features on a map

Maps use a number of features such as text, signs and symbols to provide information.

Maps usually have a title. This describes the location of the area covered by the map and may say what type of information the map shows.

Maps show direction. Most maps have a north pointer or a **compass rose** to show direction. If there is no such sign then it is assumed that north is at the top of the map.

Maps have a **key**. Labelling everything on a map would make it difficult to read. To avoid this, maps have signs and symbols drawn on them and a key which explains what the signs and symbols mean.

Maps are also drawn at different **scales**. The scale on a map is the link between a measurement on a map and the real distance on the ground.

A scale is usually shown as a line with markings at regular points which create spaces or **intervals**. This is known as a linear scale.

All of these things are known as **marginal** information.

▲ This linear scale shows that every interval on the scale is equal to 2 km on the ground.

Maps give information using words, numbers and colours. Colour makes a map easier to read but can also be used to show how the ground changes in height or different kinds of use of the land.

▲ This map shows the different information features used in a map.

3.2 Using maps 2

Location

Maps help us to locate places in the world. They help us to know the position of different countries and geographical features in relation to one another.

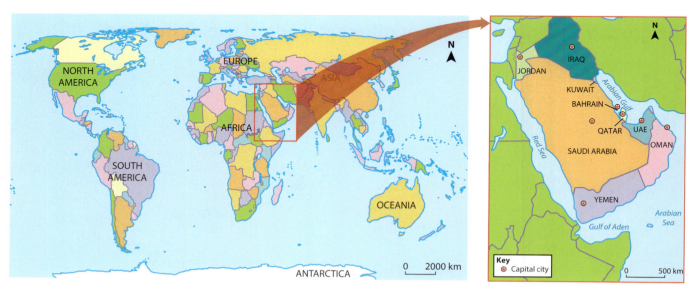

▲ A The Arabian Peninsula is in South-west Asia, close to Africa.

The Arabian Peninsula is part of a larger region sometimes called the Middle East. The region can also be described as being in South-west Asia.

Location within the region

The Arabian Peninsula has coastlines on three sides. The waters are the Red Sea to the west and the Arabian Sea to the south and south-east. To the north east is the Arabian Gulf and the Gulf of Oman with the Strait of Hormuz between them.

Size

Maps can give a clear idea of the size of countries in relation to one another. Countries of the Arabian Peninsula are very different in size as map A shows and as is clear in the table.

Country	Area (km^2)
Saudi Arabia	2,149,690
Yemen	527,970
Oman	309,500
UAE	83,600
Kuwait	17,820
Qatar	11,850
Bahrain	933

▲ Land area of some countries of the Arabian Peninsula.

Height

A **relief** map shows the 'elevation' of the land which is its height above sea level.

▲ B A relief map of the Arabian Peninsula. Areas of about the same height are given the same colour.

▲ C This relief map attempts to show what the land surface actually looks like.

The surface of the land varies across the region and within countries. There are differences in height and differences in **terrain**.

The relief map (map B) shows differences in height using colour bands from north-west to south-east.

Map C shows relief in a different way which tries to show that the height increases in certain places because there are mountains.

Activities

1 Work with a partner and ask one another questions based on the map on page 41, for example 'How many mosques can you see on the map?'

2 Use a blank map of the Arabian Peninsula to create a relief map as in map B. Mark all the capital cities.

3.3 Coordinates

In this lesson you will learn:
- to use coordinates to describe a location.

Coordinate squares

Coordinates are used to identify a position on a map. A grid of lines is drawn over the map to divide it up into squares. The coordinates are used to identify a particular square. They come in two parts. The first part tells us how far to move along the horizontal line at the bottom of a map. The second part tells us how far to move up the vertical edge.

Some simple coordinates combine letters and numbers to identify a square, as in map A. Here, the coordinates for a particular square would be a letter followed by a number, such as H,5. To find this square you trace along the bottom of the map to the letter H. You then trace up the grid from that point until you reach the row of squares in line with the number 5 at the left-hand side.

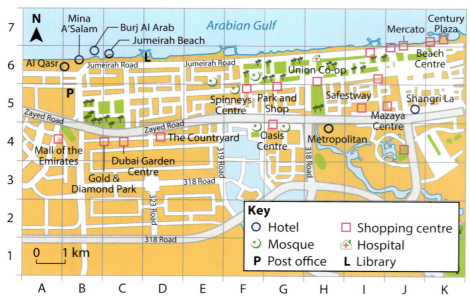

▲ **A** Simple coordinates are often used on maps designed to help people find their way around a city, for example a tourist map or a city guide, as in this map of part of Dubai.

Coordinates on gridlines

Coordinates can be based on the gridlines of a map. These are called grid references and are usually a pair of numbers.

Grid references are sometimes written in brackets and are used in the order they appear, for example (2,5). Using grid references (2,5) on map B we find the second line along from the left then up this vertically until it crosses the line next to the five. At this point we find a hospital.

On any map only a few landmarks will actually fall where two lines cross. Grid references are therefore used to identify a whole square. The grid reference refers to the square upwards and to the right of the point where the gridlines cross, as in the section shown in map C.

▲ B A simple map of part of Doha. The grid laid over the map has numbers on each of the lines.

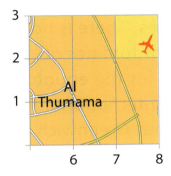

◀ C A detail of map B showing the square identified by the grid references (7,2).

Activities

1 Use map A to answer these questions.
   o Which hotel is in J,5?
   o Which shopping centre is in square A,4?
   o In which square is the Burj Al Arab?
   o Give coordinates of two separate mosques.
   o Which road runs from B,3 to E,3?

2 Working with a partner, use map B to make up some grid reference questions.

3.4 Latitude and longitude

In this lesson you will learn:
- about lines of latitude and longitude
- how to use latitude and longitude to locate places in the world.

Worldwide coordinates

Many world maps and globes have gridlines drawn on them which act as coordinates. Where the lines are drawn is based on the fact that the Earth is a sphere.

To understand why the lines are drawn in particular places we need to know that:

- the Earth is a sphere which is a 3D shape based on a circle
- the unit if measuring for angles is a degree
- the symbol for a degree is °
- a circle is divided into 360°.

Gridlines are drawn a certain number of degrees apart, as if measured from the centre of the Earth. The lines across a map or around a globe running east to west are called lines of latitude. The lines running from the north to the south are called lines of longitude.

Latitude

We imagine the Earth spinning round an axis that has a North and South Pole. The equator is a line of latitude running around the centre of the Earth and an equal distance from both Poles. It has a value of 0°.

All lines of latitude are parallel to the equator. There are 90° of latitude north of the equator and 90° south. These are 'degrees north' and 'degrees south'.

Longitude

Lines of longitude run at right-angles to lines of latitude. All of them pass through both the North and South Poles. There is no obvious starting point for lines of longitude as there is for the equator. It was agreed at an international conference in 1884 that Greenwich in London would be given the value 0°. This is called the Prime Meridian.

? If the North Pole is at 90° north, where is the South Pole?

The Earth is divided equally into 360° of longitude. There are 180° of longitude going east of the Prime Meridian ('degrees East') and 180° of longitude going west ('degrees West').

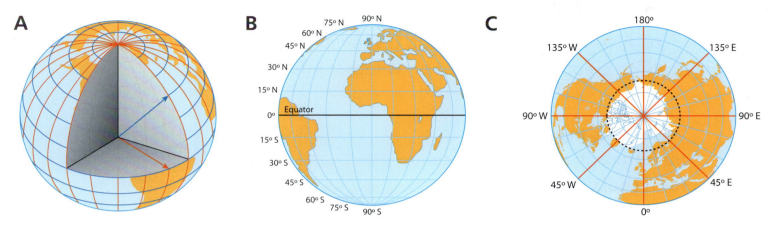

▲ **A** Lines of latitude and longitude are drawn using angles measured from the centre of the Earth. The red arrow points to a line of longitude and the blue arrow points to a line of latitude. **B** Lines of latitude are parallel to the equator. **C** A view of the world from above the North Pole.

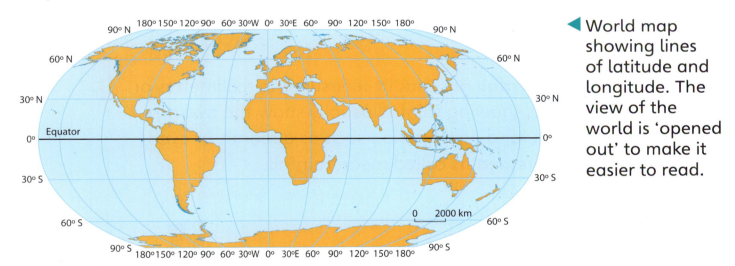

◀ World map showing lines of latitude and longitude. The view of the world is 'opened out' to make it easier to read.

Activities

Work in a group.

1 Find out or estimate the latitude and longitude of your country. Use an atlas or globe to help you.

2 Write a list of countries and oceans that are on the same line of latitude and the same line of longitude.

3.5 Rainfall charts

In this lesson you will learn:
- how weather information is shown on charts
- to create charts based on weather information.

Weather is the conditions in the atmosphere over a place for a short period of time. The main parts of the weather are **precipitation**, temperature and wind. All of these can be measured and used to describe the weather.

▲ Sometimes there is snow in the mountains of Oman and occasionally in the mountains in the north-east of the United Arab Emirates.

Rainfall

Precipitation and rainfall are usually measured in millimetres or centimetres. Charts showing rainfall usually show the average amount of rainfall for a given period such as a month or even a year. This measurement is called mean rainfall.

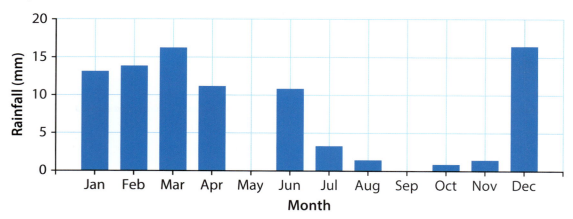

▲ This chart shows the average rainfall for each month of the year in Muscat, Oman.

Making a rainfall chart

A rainfall chart has one horizontal line or **axis** that goes across the page. The other axis is vertical and goes up the page.

The horizontal axis shows the months of the year and the vertical axis shows the amount of rainfall. This is usually measured in centimetres or millimetres. The highest value shown on the vertical axis must be at least as high as the measurement for the month with the most rain.

The vertical axis is divided into intervals. These are the spaces between the grid lines which are given a particular value, for example 5 mm, as in the rainfall chart shown here.

To make the chart, a bar is drawn for each month, up to the height of the grid line that matches the amount of rainfall as shown on the vertical axis.

The importance of precipitation

The amount of precipitation that falls has an effect on the amount of water available and so it is very important. In countries of the Arabian Gulf there is very little rainfall for most of the year. This means that any water that is available has to be used very carefully and wisely. Rainfall has an important influence on what foods can be grown and which animals can be reared.

Activities

1 Refer to the rainfall chart (opposite) to answer these questions.
   - What are the two wettest months in Muscat?
   - What are the months with least rain?
   - Which period of the year would you say possibly has the most days without rain?

2 Carry out some research to find out the average precipitation rates in your area and in a place in another part of the world. Make a chart or charts to present this information.

3.6 Temperature and wind charts

In this lesson you will learn:
- how weather information is shown on charts
- to create charts based on weather information.

Temperature

In weather terms, temperature is a measure of the hotness or coldness of the air. Temperature is most commonly measured in degrees Celsius (°C) or degrees Fahrenheit (°F). Air temperature is affected by a number of things, especially the amount of sunshine. Places with clear skies and hours of strong sunshine are warmer. The sun's rays are stronger nearer the equator and so temperatures are higher.

Temperature charts

Charts showing temperature can be bar charts or line graphs.

Temperature charts often show the average highest temperature and the average lowest temperature for each month. This means that people can be quite confident that the actual temperature in those months will be between these values.

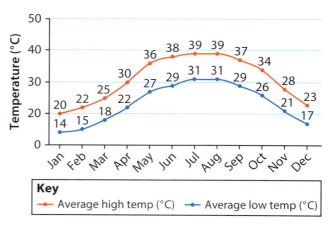

▲ Average maximum and minimum temperatures, Manama, Bahrain.

The importance of temperature

High temperatures can cause dehydration, heat exhaustion or heatstroke in people. Temperature affects human activity such as farming.

Wind

Wind is air that moves as a result of natural forces. The direction from which the air comes is important.

When air travels over water it picks up moisture which can fall as rain. When air travels over land it remains dry and will bring no rain. Wind brings cool air if it travels from a cool place and warm air if it travels from somewhere warm.

Wind direction is described using the direction from which the wind has come. A 'south-east wind' blows *from* the south-east. The strength of the wind is another important part of this weather feature.

◀ Average wind speed km/h in Doha, Qatar.

The importance of wind

Wind can be a gentle cooling breeze or part of a dangerous storm. In countries in the Arabian Gulf an important type of wind is known as the Shamal. A Shamal can bring gusty winds, sand and dust storms and heavy seas. All of these can have a negative effect on transport and other human activity.

▲ Sand or dust storms reduce visibility and make travelling more dangerous.

Activities

1 Find out about the average temperatures in your local area.

2 Find out about recent local events caused by winds and write a brief report.

3.7 Water resources

In this lesson you will learn:
- about the water resources of countries in the Arabian Gulf.

Water exists as surface water in streams, rivers, lakes and seas. It can also be stored naturally under the ground as **groundwater.** Water is a scarce resource in countries in the Arabian Gulf because they are in an arid climate zone where there is very little rainfall.

Water is used for human consumption and **sanitation**, for agriculture and in industry.

Water underground

When water falls as rain in countries of the Arabian Gulf, most of it **evaporates** back into the air. Some runs off the land into streams or rivers and some soaks into the ground. Areas of rock that are able to hold water underground are called **aquifers**. These are the main source of water for most countries in the Arabian Gulf. The level at which water can be found underground is called the **water table**.

Problems arise if water is taken faster than it is replaced. If water is not being replaced at all then it will run out completely.

Underground water can also become salty which means it is not good to drink and cannot be used for irrigating plants.

Oases

Oases are found where water comes to the surface in a desert landscape. An oasis will support vegetation and wildlife. Larger oases will

▲ People in the region have been drawing water from underground using wells for thousands of years.

also support human life and even allow for permanent settlements.

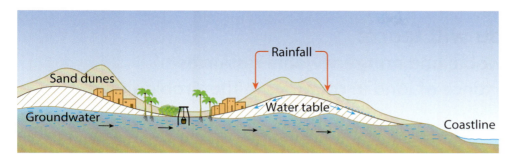

> **Did you know?**
> The largest aquifer in Saudi Arabia is full of water that collected 20,000 years ago.

Key
→ Groundwater travels through from the dunes down to underlying rock
→ Direction of flow of water underground

▲ Oases are places where underground water is at or near the surface of the ground. Examples of large oases are Al-Hasa in eastern Saudi Arabia and the Liwa and Al-Ayn oases in the United Arab Emirates.

Dams

Dams are structures built across a *wadi*, to trap and store water as it flows downhill. When it rains, the dry channel of the wadi fills with water.

There are important dams in mountainous areas of Oman, in the north-east of the United Arab Emirates and in Saudi Arabia.

In some places water is carried from the dams in a system of channels and tunnels to the places where it is needed.

▲ Stores of water behind dams are called reservoirs.

Water from the sea

Another source of water is the sea. Sea water is salty and so the salt must be taken out before it can be drunk. This is done in a process called **desalination**. Desalinated water is expensive to produce.

Activity

Work in a group to make a brief presentation about one source of water in your country.

3.8 Renewable or non-renewable?

In this lesson you will learn:
- to identify renewable and non-renewable resources
- about the importance of land in countries in the Arabian Gulf.

Natural resources

Natural resources are any material or feature from the natural world that people are able to use to meet their needs.

We live on land which makes it an important natural resource. We use it for many different purposes including agriculture, housing and transportation. We use other natural resources as **raw materials** to make other materials and items, or to use as fuel.

Some natural resources are renewable. These are the ones that are always freely available, such as sunshine, or those that will be replaced naturally over a period of time. Trees, other plants and fish are examples of renewable resources that replace themselves naturally.

▲ Today's technology means that the heat from the sun can be used to generate electricity.

Other resources are **non-renewable**. These are the ones that are not replaced by nature and which will therefore eventually run out. Non-renewable resources include substances such as oil, metals, stone and rock.

An important idea in the use of resources is **sustainability**. If something is sustained it means it lasts a long time. Sustainability of resources is about using and managing them well so that they last or are not destroyed.

Land

The surface of the land can be put to different uses. There is pressure on the land to provide space for people to live but also to provide many of the resources they need such as food. An important use of land has always been the production of food. A challenge facing many countries in the Arabian Gulf is to provide enough food for a very fast-growing **population**.

This is especially difficult for two reasons. Firstly, much of the land within these countries is not naturally suitable for growing crops. It is low in nutrients and drains quickly so those nutrients are washed away. Secondly, agriculture uses large amounts of water, but these countries have very limited resources.

◀ Many different food crops are grown.

Great efforts have been made to increase production but large amounts of food still have to be imported from other countries.

Other areas of land need to be used to build towns and cities to provide places for people to live and work. These areas are also needed for education, education services, business and industry.

▲ It is important that areas that are naturally very beautiful are left that way for everyone to enjoy.

Some areas of the land are beautiful to look at and for this reason they are an important resource. They give people pleasure and are popular for visiting and **sightseeing**. Some of these places act as attractions for **tourists**.

Activity

Draw and write about four different uses of land in your country.

3.9 Oil, gas and minerals

In this lesson you will learn:
- the uses of oil and gas
- about the importance of oil and gas to countries in the Arabian Gulf.

Oil

Oil and gas are known as fossil fuels and are non-renewable resources. The countries of the Arabian Gulf are among the world's largest producers of oil and natural gas.

Oil from the ground is called crude oil. Crude oil is processed to make fuels for different types of transport and for industry.

Products from oil are important in almost every industry on Earth and products made from oil include plastics. waxes, medicines, **fertilisers** and **cosmetics**.

Oil products are an important part of almost every industry on Earth. Items made using products from crude oil include plastics, waxes, medicines, fertilisers and cosmetics.

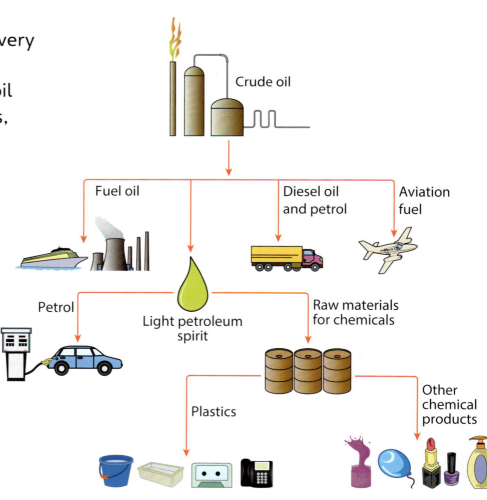

▲ A huge range of products are made from crude oil.

Gas

Natural gas is useful mainly because it burns easily and releases a lot of heat energy. It is used in heating and cooking in homes and in large power stations to create electricity.

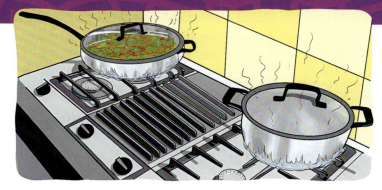
▲ Many kitchens have cookers that burn natural gas.

Burning fossil fuels creates pollution and it is important for people to think about how they use these resources and the products that are made from them.

Minerals

Minerals are naturally occurring solid substances, such as rock. Rocks of various kinds have many different uses.

Some rocks are very attractive and used as decoration in buildings. Other rocks can be used to create artworks.

Some rocks, such as limestone, are used in making products like cement, while other rocks are simply broken up and used to make roads and concrete.

Some rocks, known as 'ores', contain metals such as copper, gold and iron. **Bauxite** is an ore found in Saudi Arabia which provides the material to make aluminium.

Non-metallic minerals found in the Arabian Gulf countries include limestone, marble and **gypsum**.

Activity

Work in a group to produce an information poster about renewable and non-renewable resources.

▲ Aluminium is used to make many different products.

3.10 Resources from the sea

In this lesson you will learn:
- about the vegetation that grows naturally in the Arabian Gulf
- to identify resources available from trees and other plants
- to identify the wild animals of the region
- about the resources available from the sea.

Natural vegetation

Natural vegetation is all the plants and trees that grow in the wild. The region has a very dry climate and the soil is often of poor quality. Although much of the land area of some countries is covered with desert, there are many different **habitats** where plants are able to live.

In some coastal regions there are some permanently flooded areas called salt marshes. Mangrove trees are able to survive here and they provide a habitat for many species of fish, other animals and birds.

Various small flowering plants and shrubs grow in other places, together with a range of grasses. Although some plants have been used in history as sources of food or medicine, they are most useful as a resource because they provide food for **grazing** animals. They are also a part of the natural systems in the region and help to support the wildlife that lives here.

A variety of trees grow in the region and some of the larger ones are good nesting sites for birds. Trees have been used in the past to provide wood for burning or to make **charcoal**. Some species provide fruit; the most common example is the date palm. Date palms

▲ The Sidr tree grows freely in hilly areas, especially around rocky wadis and provides edible fruit. Many other parts of the tree are used for **medicinal** purposes. Bees collect nectar from the trees' flowers and make the valuable Sidr honey.

grow best in places where there is a good supply of water so they are usually found near oases. In Oman, special types of trees are the source of incense.

Wildlife

In the past some wildlife was hunted for food. People would train falcons to catch small animals such as hares or birds, including the houbara. This is the origin of the sport of falconry.

Today, although the tradition of falconry continues, most wildlife in the area of the Arabian Gulf is protected and recognised as a valuable resource for a different reason. The beautiful and sometimes very rare creatures are a popular attraction for visitors and tourists. There are several special areas where animals are protected and a number of wildlife parks have been created.

▲ Wild creatures are a popular attraction for tourists and local visitors.

Fish and sea creatures

Fish have been an important source of food for centuries and this is still true today. The main fishing grounds are in the waters of the Arabian Gulf, the Gulf of Oman and the Arabian Sea. These environments are also home to other **marine** life, including endangered species such as the green turtle and the dugong. This marine life is also a valuable resource because it forms part of the attraction for recreational diving, a popular activity with tourists.

The Gulf waters also have oyster beds which produce natural pearls. These are still a valuable resource.

Activity

Create a diagram that shows the resources available from plants, animals and the sea.

3.11 Population

In these lessons you will learn:
- why information about a population is useful
- to make a population chart
- who makes up the population of countries in the Arabian Gulf.

Population data

The population is the number of people living in a given area. Population **statistics** provide information including the number of people living in a country, numbers in different areas within a country and numbers in major settlements.

Knowing the number of people in a population helps people to know about the amount of resources required to meet a population's needs. When a country's population grows very quickly, it can be difficult to keep up with the demand for things such as fresh water and food.

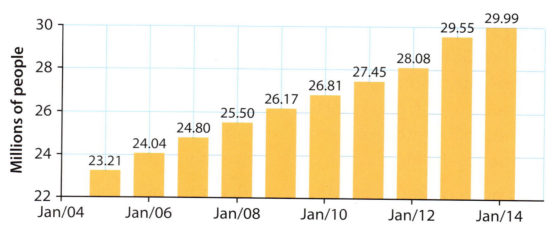

▲ Chart of population growth in Saudi Arabia.

A population is also studied to identify the different groups of people within it and the effects this might have. For example, the balance of males and females in a population at different ages can affect the number of marriages. This can affect the number of children who might be born.

The number of people in different age groups in a population is known as the age structure. It is useful to know about this because people have different needs and require different resources, especially in terms of education, health and housing, depending on their age.

Different groups

The native populations in countries of the Arabian Gulf are Arabs who are descended from different tribes in the region. Groups of people with a different heritage and from different countries have lived in the region for a very long time but many more people have moved to live in the area in recent times.

The discovery of oil in various countries of the Arabian Gulf in the mid-20th century provided great wealth. The governments wanted to spend this money helping their countries to develop. This involved a great deal of construction work and the creation of modern services such as health and education. The work available in all these areas brought Arab and non-Arab people from many countries to live in this area.

The largest non-Arab groups are from Southern and South-east Asian countries such as India, Pakistan, Bangladesh, Indonesia and the Philippines. Smaller groups include people from Europe and North America.

Activities

1 Work in a group to research the population of your country and how this has changed over time. Make a chart to present what you find out.

2 Work in a group to find out about the groups of people from different cultures and countries who live in your country. Find and mark the country of origin of the different groups on a world map.

3.12 People and places

In this lesson you will learn:
- where people live within countries of the Arabian Gulf
- to identify the relationships between land use and the location of settlements
- about life in a city and in a village.

Did you know?
By 2014 there were more than 24 million people living in Shanghai in China. This means that it is the city with the largest population in the world.

Where people live

A settlement is a place where people live. In the past in Arabian Gulf countries some settlements have been temporary because the people were nomads and did not stay in one place. People who were animal herders lived in areas where the land provided food for their animals.

Permanent settlements began where people had access to fresh water and food. They grew food crops or reared animals and on the coast they could fish. Places on trade routes also became established and grew with the trade.

◀ This map of the United Arab Emirates shows how many of today's modern towns and cities are in areas where past settlements would have been able to develop.

The growth of towns and cities

Permanent settlements include towns, cities and villages. Towns and cities are large settlements which create what are known as urban areas. Urban areas have a large population and the environment is mostly built up by the people who live there.

▲ Large amounts of fish from the Arabian Gulf are still landed in fishing villages.

Areas away from urban areas are known as rural. In rural areas the environment is more natural and there is less evidence of human activity and fewer buildings. Villages are smaller settlements found in rural areas. These are often centred round an oasis, where a crop such as date palms will grow, or on the coast, where fishing is an important activity.

In the past, an older settlement probably had one main purpose. It may have been a port, a fishing village or a market. Some places were stopping points on an important trade route. As a settlement grew other kinds of activity would also develop. A wide range of things happen in modern cities and there are areas for shopping, business and industry and people's needs for education and healthcare are also met.

It is partly for these reasons that many people want to live in cities. Across the world, the proportion of people living in urban areas is increasing. The great majority of the populations in the countries of the Arabian Gulf live in cities.

Knowing where people live is important for governments and planners because it helps them to know where money needs to be spent.

Activities

1 Work with a partner to discuss the settlement you live in and why it is located in its current position.

2 Work in a group to make a presentation about the different things available in a modern city in your country.

Unit 3 Review questions

1. In geography, the word 'region' is best described as an area of the Earth:
   a. where different places have some similar characteristics
   b. where countries share borders
   c. where countries have coastlines on the same body of water
   d. where people all speak the same language

2. A relief map shows:
   a. bodies of water
   b. where people live
   c. the height of land above sea level
   d. different levels of population

3. Coordinates on a map help us to:
   a. hold the map in the correct way
   b. know the direction in which to travel between two places on the map
   c. know the distance between two places on the map
   d. locate features and places on the map

4. An aquifer is:
   a. a system used for irrigating crops
   b. an area of underground rock that can hold water
   c. a small dam for storing water
   d. a hole dug into the ground to collect water

5. Write about two renewable resources and two non-renewable resources that are available in the Arabian Gulf.

6. Describe two ways in which information about the size of the population in a country might be useful for the government.

7. Briefly describe how the populations of Arabian Gulf countries have changed since the middle of the 20th century.

8. Describe some of the similarities and differences between the reasons people in the past chose where to live and the reasons people have today.

4 Citizenship

In this unit you will learn:
- that all people, including children, have rights
- about the environment and how to care for it
- how and why people communicate
- about the government, laws, the economy
- how people make a living and spend their money
- to design a public information campaign.

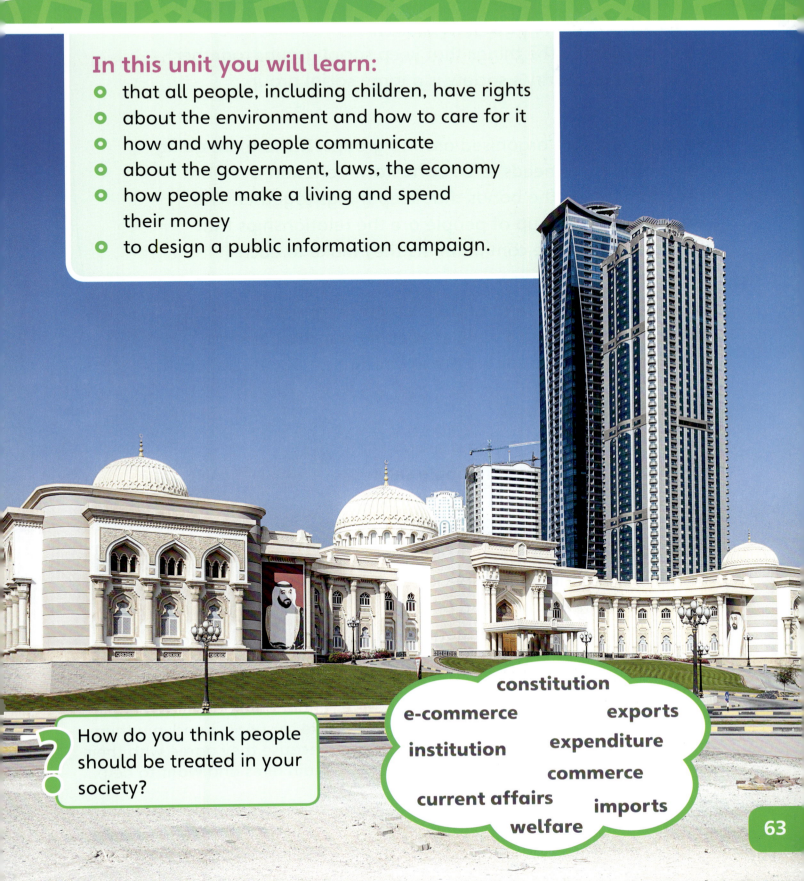

? How do you think people should be treated in your society?

constitution
e-commerce
exports
institution
expenditure
commerce
current affairs
imports
welfare

4.1 Social groups and society

In this lesson you will learn:
- to identify the things that keep social groups together
- that a country's society is a large social group.

People's lives are organised around groups. If these are going to succeed there needs to be **cohesion**. Cohesion is a word used to describe the bonds that keep things together. The bonds within a group of people are the relationships that they create and the commitments they make to each other and to the group.

Although we make relationships and form groups naturally, We sometimes have to work at keeping our relationships positive and the groups we are in strong.

A common goal

People usually want to join a group because of its purpose. If people see that a group is achieving its goal then they will stay committed. A group can form with a very specific aim, such as saving an endangered species of animal, or a more general aim such as building community relationships.

The society of a country has a number of wide-reaching goals such as creating peace and security and allowing the people who live in it to do their best.

▲ Many groups exist to protect endangered animals. People like to support and join them because they agree with their main aims and want to help.

Control

There needs to be control within a group so that it is able to achieve its goals. The attitudes and behaviour of members of the group need to be controlled so that relationships within the group stay positive and strong. Control within a group is achieved through the use of rules and regulations.

Leadership

The leaders of a group are responsible for deciding what the aims of the group should be. In a friendship group this happens quite informally and there may be a lot of discussion. In more formal groups people in leadership are able to make decisions on behalf of other group members. The leaders may decide on certain actions that need to be taken and can organise other members to see that the aims of the group are achieved.

◀ Sports teams have captains who can make decisions about what happens and how the game should be played.

Authority

Authority is the right to do something. In a group, the leaders are given the authority to make decisions on behalf of the group and to ask other people in the group to do certain things. Group members are usually happy to co-operate with this provided that the things they are expected to do are reasonable.

Activity

Think about a group to which you belong and write two sentences for each of the following headings: Common goal, Control, Leadership, Authority.

4.2 Behaviour in society

In this lesson you will learn:
- to identify ways in which people are expected to behave in Arabian Gulf societies.

Cultural traditions

Cultural traditions give a society its sense of identity and are an important part of helping a society to hold together. The countries of the Arabian Gulf are Arab Muslim societies. This means that they are based on Arab traditions and the faith of Islam.

The family is at the centre of Arab society. The family is the main place in which cultural and social traditions are handed down. It gives people a feeling of safety and offers support to individual members. For all these reasons the family is highly regarded and members of society are expected to behave in ways that respect and strengthen the family. The family's reputation in society is also important.

Other values and traditions shared by Arab societies include hospitality and generosity. There is also a strong sense of solidarity within groups of friends and neighbours. Islam teaches respect and tolerance and the importance of the family.

Improving society

A person who wants to be a good member of a society will be aware of things that are happening in society. This means that they will not be completely self-centred but will be thinking about the needs, feelings and rights of others. They will also see things in society that need improving and will do something about them.

◀ We all have a responsibility to care for others in our society.

Each day we have the opportunity to affect other people and society. We can have a positive influence simply by behaving with kindness and openness towards others. It is also important to remember people who are in a situation that makes life more difficult, such as older people, for example.

Each person can help to make a society one in which there is a caring attitude towards all people and especially those in need.

Unacceptable behaviour

Behaviour that is socially unacceptable or anti-social shows lack of consideration for other people's needs and feelings and damages a society.

Activities

1. Write a brief explanation of why you think values such as hospitality, generosity, respect and tolerance would help to create a strong society.
2. Work in a group to discuss ways in which pupils can contribute to the life of a school.

4.3 Human rights

In this lesson you will learn:
- about human rights
- how human rights affect society.

Needs and rights

People have basic needs such as food, clothes and water. These are the things they need in order to survive. If they are going to do more than just survive, people need other things too. They need:

- to feel loved and accepted
- to feel safe and secure
- to be educated so that they can do their best

> **Did you know?**
> The Arabian Gulf countries of Kuwait, Bahrain, Saudi Arabia, Qatar, United Arab Emirates and Oman are among the 193 members of the United Nations.

- access to medicines that can stop them becoming ill
- medical care to help them if they are already suffering from an illness or are injured.

As modern societies developed they moved beyond a situation where the main concern was survival. People came to see that everyone in the world should have all their basic needs met in terms of having enough food, water and shelter. They also began to think that everyone has a right to feel loved and safe, and that people should get access to education as well as medical care.

These rights were felt to apply to all human beings. They are therefore called human rights.

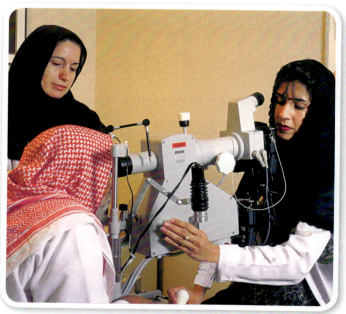

▲ The Declaration of Human Rights says that everyone is entitled to the healthcare they need.

International law and human rights

The United Nations is an organisation which is made up of representatives of countries from around the world. The United Nations is committed to maintaining international peace and security. It develops friendly relations between countries and promotes better living standards and social conditions for everyone.

In 1948, the United Nations drew up a special piece of international law called the Universal Declaration of Human Rights. This was intended to set out and **guarantee** the rights of every individual everywhere.

The declaration says that everyone is entitled to the rights it contains regardless of:

- whether they are male or female
- the colour of their skin
- the language they speak
- the ideas they have
- the religion they follow
- the amount of wealth they have
- the social group to which they belong
- the country they come from.

Many other articles in the declaration explain other rights that people have, including those of personal safety and freedom.

◀ The Declaration of Human Rights always makes it clear that everyone has the same rights simply because they are human.

The 10th December every year is Human Rights Day and marks the anniversary of the presentation of the Universal Declaration of Human Rights.

Activity

Make a poster to inform people about the Universal Declaration of Human Rights or Human Rights Day.

4.4 Children's rights

In this lesson you will learn:
- about special human rights that apply to children.

Children's experiences

We know that when children are born they are completely helpless and need other people to provide for all their needs. As they grow they learn to do more things for themselves and develop their own personalities. They still need to have most things provided for them. They also need protection and other help to keep them safe.

Children's lives are very different in countries around the world. They are often expected to take an active role in helping within their families and communities. In some societies this means doing simple chores around the house. In other societies it means walking a long way to fetch water or to collect wood for a cooking fire. In some societies children are expected to help in a family business such as a farm, even if this means that they cannot go to school.

Children's rights

The fact that children have special rights was made clear in another piece of International Law called the Convention on the Rights of the Child. This was written in 1989 and came into force in 1990. It set out special rights that all children have.

The law laid out what children were allowed to do and believe. The law speaks about children's right to develop to the best of their ability. For this to happen it is felt that children need to be able to go to school. The Convention says that children have the right to go to a good school and should be encouraged to study to the highest level they can.

◀ It is still true today that millions of children do not receive a primary school education.

The Convention made it clear that the people who are responsible for children have to make sure that those children are happy, healthy and safe.

The Convention also states 'children have a right to relax, play and join in a wide range of cultural and artistic activities'.

▲ Children need to be able to join in with a wide range of activities.

Activity

Research some of the articles of the Convention on the Rights of the Child. Choose two and prepare a presentation for the class that explains them.

4.5 The local environment

In this lesson you will learn:
- to identify different areas of the local environment
- to identify threats to the local environment and action that can be taken to protect it.

The local environment

The local environment is made up of all the physical features we see on the land around us both natural and built by people. It also includes all water bodies, such as the seas, inlets and lakes, and the air.

Natural physical features

Natural physical features are parts of the environment which exist naturally. On land, these include features such as beaches, hills and valleys and the vegetation that grows in these places.

The waters of the Arabian Gulf are an important feature, together with the different environments they contain such as coral reefs. Along the coasts are features such as cliffs and beaches. All these environments are the habitats of many types of plant and animal life.

▲ Coral reefs provide a very special habitat for plants and animals.

The built environment

All the permanent structures and landscapes made by people are features of the built environment. In a city these features include houses, office blocks, factories, transportation systems and 'public spaces' such as city squares and public parks.

Outside the city, the built environment includes the roads that connect different places and structures such as dams.

The air

We are all aware of the importance of clean air to people. Breathing polluted air can cause serious harm to people's health. This also applies to all other air-breathing animals. What is less obvious is damage caused to plants and vegetation by being exposed to polluted air. Plants affected by air pollution may not grow as much as they should and if they are plants that bear fruit or are grown for crops, then they may produce less than if they were healthy.

Threats to the environment

Land pollution occurs when people do not deal properly with litter and when there are spillages of oil or chemicals. Similar problems cause pollution to the waters of the Arabian Gulf. This is a particular problem because marine environments are especially sensitive.

The air is polluted by the gases coming from transport vehicles and from many other industrial processes such as oil refining, energy production and quarrying.

▲ The built environment has grown quickly in Arabian Gulf countries.

Activity

Work in a group. Read the paragraph *Threats to the environment* again and identify areas in your local environment which could be polluted or damaged in some other way.

◀ We have to balance our need for energy and industry with the effects on the environment.

4.6 Practical local action

In this lesson you will learn:
- to explain why everyone has a responsibility towards the local environment
- to identify environmental issues in the local environment
- about local initiatives.

Shared responsibility

We live in groups with other people and we are all part of a large society. For these reasons we have to think about the feelings and rights of other people. We must be aware that our actions have consequences for other people.

We share the local natural and built environments and so we share the responsibility for them too. Clean and tidy environments are healthier and nicer to look at and so one of our responsibilities is to help keep them clean.

We first learn about the importance of cleanliness in our homes. We also learn that we should not simply rely on other people to clean up after us.

Waste management

Human activity produces waste. More people living in an area means a larger amount of waste produced. The systems that are put in place to deal with the waste get larger and more complicated.

In large cities the **municipal authority** is responsible for organising a system of waste management. The system includes waste collection from homes, offices, schools and shopping malls. Public areas are provided with bins into which people can place litter. When people do not dispose of litter correctly and do not use the bins provided, waste problems occur in the open environment, outside homes and buildings.

▲ Municipal authorities provide litter bins in public places.

Reducing waste

As the population in an area grows, more and more waste is produced. As a result, it is important that each person tries to reduce the amount of waste that he or she produces.

People can:

- reduce the waste they create by only buying the things they need, buying items that can be re-used and items that come with little or no packaging. Unwanted items that are still usable can be given away to other people
- re-use items before they are eventually disposed of which makes better use of the resource. Many everyday items such as carrier bags, glass jars and paper can be re-used in different ways
- recycle materials such as paper, glass and metals such as steel and aluminium. Recycling is a process that turns waste materials into new products.

Activity

Work in a group to design a campaign that encourages people to reduce waste, re-use and recycle.

4.7 Personal communications

In this lesson you will learn:
- about different types of personal communication
- when it is appropriate to use different types of personal communication.

Personal communication takes places when people, as individuals or in groups, communicate directly. Developing **interpersonal** skills helps to ensure good communication.

◀ We use interpersonal skills all the time, without really thinking about it.

Good interpersonal skills include communication, negotiation and assertiveness. These skills help people form and maintain strong personal relationships. They also help as people deal with others in their family and friendship groups, in school and at work.

Verbal communication

Spoken verbal communication is made up of the words we say. What we say must make sense and communicate the information we want to get across. Just as important is the way we speak and the tone of voice we use.

Non-verbal communication

Non-verbal communication is all the parts of communication that happen without words. This includes body language, facial expressions, eye contact and sometimes touching, as in a hand shake.

Listening skills

Listening is the ability to accurately receive and interpret messages. Failure to listen well means that messages are easily misunderstood and good communication does not happen. Effective listening requires focus and paying attention to all the communication that is taking place, verbally and non-verbally.

▲ We receive a lot of information through non-verbal communication.

Negotiation

Negotiation is a process that people use to try to settle differences and avoid arguments. People negotiate in order to reach a solution to a problem that is fair, that each person is happy with and which maintains the relationship.

Assertiveness

Assertiveness is the ability to express your thoughts, feelings and beliefs in an honest and open way. It is about standing up for your right to hold and express those ideas. Being assertive is not the same as being aggressive. An assertive response or communication always respects the thoughts, feelings, beliefs and rights of others.

Activities

1. Work with a partner. Tell your partner about the different members in your family, your favourite food, favourite colour and something you really like to do. Your partner should listen carefully. Then swap and you listen to your partner. Both of you must be ready to feed back to the class what your partner has said.

2. Make a list of situations in which you use different interpersonal skills and explain how you communicate.

4.8 Mass media

In this lesson you will learn:
- what is meant by mass media
- the functions of mass media.

When we talk about the media in terms of communication we refer to all the different means by which people can communicate. When an organisation or an institution communicates over a wide area and to a lot (or mass) of people, it uses 'mass media'.

Familiar forms of printed mass media are newspapers and magazines, posters and leaflets. Electronic mass media include television, radio and the internet.

Mass media exists to:

- provide information and comment on **current affairs**
- keep citizens informed and help them to make judgments
- educate people through documentaries and discussions
- provide entertainment.

Newspapers

Newspapers often have different sections which focus on news and current affairs, business, sport and arts and culture. They cover events both within a country and in other parts of the world.

Magazines

Magazines are another form of print media. They are usually published less frequently than a newspaper and are often aimed at a particular section of the population, for example children. They can also have a particular focus, such as computers, cars or fashion.

▲ People rely on daily newspapers to keep them informed of important events.

Television and radio

Television and radio make up the 'broadcast media' which means that the programmes they prepare are transmitted from one place to other places where they can be received.

Early television and radio programmes made by different companies were originally transmitted from tall masts located on the ground. The radio and television signals were not very strong and there was a limit to how far they could travel. As a result, only a limited amount of people had access to broadcast media. Today the programmes are often transmitted along special cables or via a satellite. Events in different places around the world can be watched almost anywhere. We can often watch events 'live', as they are happening.

◄ Many broadcast programmes are transmitted by satellite.

The internet

The internet has changed the way mass media works. Many newspapers have a version available online and television and radio can be accessed through a computer or mobile phone. The internet also allows individuals to **post** written material or images online.

Mass media ownership

Mass media can be operated and controlled by private companies or by a government.

Activity

Work in a group to carry out a survey of types of mass media in your country. Make a list of the different types of information presented.

4.9 Public information

In this lesson you will learn:
- what is meant by public information
- the purpose of public information.

Public information campaigns

Public information campaigns are run by authorities in the **public sector** with the purpose of informing and changing the behaviour of large numbers of people. The campaigns usually encourage actions and behaviour that would be good for individuals and for society. Campaigns use a range of media and will often be planned to run over a set period of time.

Health promotion

A major area of public information campaigning is to do with promoting the health of individuals and of the population in general. People's health is often linked to their lifestyle and so a campaign on this issue will address such things as diet and exercise.

A health campaign might inform the public about the benefits of eating a healthy diet, what makes a healthy diet and how to create that diet. It may focus on the benefits of regular exercise and give advice on recommended activities.

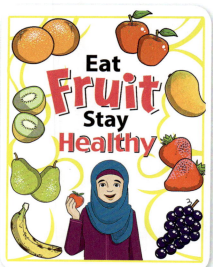

▲ Many health campaigns are aimed at improving people's health.

Disease prevention

A related area of public information campaigning is to do with preventing disease. These campaigns can have a number of messages. Different campaigns will:

- highlight the dangers associated with particular practices, such as smoking

- focus on diet, pointing out the problems associated with eating too much fat, salt or sugar
- alert people to diseases caused by food poisoning, informing them of the correct way to prepare and cook food
- tell people about the importance of hygiene in preventing the spread of diseases.

Health authorities also run campaigns to inform people about programmes of **immunisation**.

Safety

Important public information campaigns are to do with safety. People will be alerted to safety issues, for example concerning dangers from too much exposure to the sun, or road safety.

The authorities run public health and safety campaigns because they have a duty to care for citizens and others living in a country. Issues connected to health and injuries are also important because they affect the amount of money that a country has to spend on its health and emergency services. People's health also affects their ability to work and earn money.

▲ Posters are a useful means of passing on safety information.

The environment

Authorities also campaign to inform the public about environmental issues and to encourage people to behave in ways that respect the environment.

Activities

1 Work in a group to find out about some recent public information campaigns in your country.
2 Work in a group to design a public information campaign on a subject of your choice.

4.10 Advertising

In this lesson you will learn:
- what is meant by advertising
- the purpose of advertising
- to assess the impact of advertising.

In business and trade some people produce goods and others provide services. The people who buy these are consumers.

Business advertising is about drawing consumers' attention to a particular product or service. Special items called advertisements are placed in newspapers and magazines and on **billboards** and **digital signboards**. Advertisements are also shown on television and radio broadcasts and on the internet.

Features of printed advertisements

Advertisements are meant to draw people's attention so they are designed to be attractive. Bright colours and large lettering are used in combination with interesting or exciting images.

The words may provide some information about the product or service being offered. The language will also be used to persuade the person reading it of the benefits of buying the product or service. Advertisements also sometimes provide information about prices and special offers.

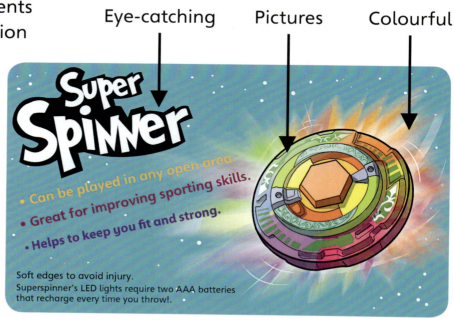

▲ Advertisements inform people about a product and also try to persuade them to buy it.

Features of television and radio advertisements

Advertisements on the radio and television have to get their message across in a very short amount of time. Radio advertisements rely on sounds and words only. The words are chosen very carefully and the way the words are spoken is very important, depending on how advertisers want people to feel. Sound effects and music can be also used to help create a particular feeling. Television adverts are able to use images as well as sound. Digital signboards are like a television screen and can show similar content.

The internet makes it possible to watch and listen to many types of advertisement.

Advantages and disadvantages of advertising

Advertising is useful when it lets people know about particular products and services they need. It can alert people to special offers and bargains which may make the product or service more affordable. Advertising is also used by organisations such as charities to let people know about the causes they support and to encourage people to donate.

Advertisements are also intended to influence people's desire to buy something or to choose one product instead of another. This can be a problem if people are encouraged to buy goods they cannot afford or to choose products that are not good for them, such as high-fat foods.

Activities

1. Work in a group to discuss products you are aware of and how these are advertised.
2. Keep a record of all the different types of advertising that you see in a week.

4.11 Government

In this lesson you will learn:
- what is meant by government
- the role of government.

Did you know?
The government puts policies in place to direct the development of different parts of a country. A government will also want the development of the country to happen in a way that does not damage the environment.

The government

To govern is to control or guide the actions of people and systems in order to achieve a particular goal or aim.

A country's national government is the group of people who have been given the authority to govern a country. This means that the government has certain powers which it can use to guide and direct the actions of people and to create and run institutions.

A government can take many forms, such as a **monarchy**, **democracy** or a **republic**. Oman, the United Arab Emirates, Qatar, Bahrain, Kuwait and Saudi Arabia are all monarchies. The monarchs are supported by other people who work in different groups within the government called **councils** and **ministries**.

◀ Governments meet in special buildings such as this one in Muscat, Oman.

The role of government

A country's government is responsible for national matters including education, health, defence, law and order, foreign policy and the environment. The government aims to create a stable society in which people feel safe and secure. People can then develop and achieve their best. Some people can provide for themselves by working and the government creates a situation where there are jobs for people to do. Other people are not so able to provide for themselves for different reasons. The government has to make sure these people have all they need too because it is responsible for the wellbeing and **welfare** of all citizens.

Governments should protect the rights of all citizens and show special care towards the **vulnerable** members of society.

The tools of government

To achieve its aims a government creates **policies**. The government can exercise power to see that certain things happen. In most cases this is done by making laws. The government will also have a system that makes sure that laws are followed.

Local government

Arabian Gulf countries are divided up into smaller areas called **municipalities** or **governorates**. The local governments of these areas focus on the needs of local people. In the United Arab Emirates, each emirate is still governed by its own ruler and has its own governments and courts.

▲ Local governments are responsible for many things including roads and transport, housing and street cleaning.

Activities

1. Find out about the government of your country.
2. Make a list of things you think the local government does to keep your area looking its best. Suggest any other things that you think they should do.

4.12 Laws

In this lesson you will learn:
- what laws are
- why laws are needed
- who makes the law
- about sanctions.

Laws

Laws are part of a system of rules and regulations within a country. They are there to guide and regulate people's actions. People should understand that the law can be enforced and that there are consequences for not obeying the law.

Why we need laws

Laws help to make it possible for many people to live together in a society. Laws help to bind a society together because they are the same for everyone and they help to create order. There are laws about behaviour, laws to protect property and to keep people safe and laws to protect people's rights.

Who makes the laws?

The main law-making body in a country is the government.

Most countries have a document called a **constitution**. This is the foundation of all the laws and lays down the principles and ideas that guide all other law-making. The constitution cannot contain all the laws that need to be written over time but each and every law has to fit in with the basic ideas within the constitution.

In countries of the Arabian Gulf the laws are guided by the principles of Islam. In many countries, some parts of the law are covered by **Sharia law**.

Some important laws

Laws prevent people behaving in ways that can cause other people harm or offence.

Many laws about food and traffic are designed to keep people safe. Food laws cover things such as how food is produced, stored and prepared. Places where food is prepared and cooked can be inspected to make sure that they are clean and hygienic so that customers who buy and eat the food do not get sick. Traffic laws include things like speed limits and other measures which encourage people to drive in a safe way.

▲ Traffic laws are designed to keep everybody safe on the roads.

Laws about property mean that no one can take what belongs to another person.

Other important laws protect people's rights and prevent them from being treated unfairly for any reason.

Sanctions

Sanctions are the things that happen when people break the law. They include having certain privileges taken away or paying a fine. Sanctions are intended to encourage people to obey the law.

Activity

Work in a group to make a presentation about laws in your country. Use the information in this book and some examples of actual laws.

4.13 The economy 1

In these lessons you will learn:
- what is meant by the economy
- about the economy in countries of the Arabian Gulf.

All societies have an economy. This is all the **goods** and **services** that are produced and used within a society. The economy also includes all the money available for people, businesses and institutions to buy the things they need.

The economy has three parts called the primary, secondary and tertiary **sectors**.

The primary sector

The primary sector is involved with providing raw materials. It includes agriculture, fishing, and industries that take resources from the ground, such as quarrying and mining.

Agriculture is a vital industry because it provides food for the people of a country. Countries of the region grow a wide range of crops including:

- fruit, including dates, citrus fruits and mangoes
- vegetables, such as cabbage, tomatoes, cucumbers, aubergines, beans and pumpkins
- cereals, such as wheat and corn.

The keeping and rearing of **livestock** animals is another important part of agriculture. These animals are reared to provide meat or for other products such as eggs and milk.

Governments of Arabian Gulf countries are keen to increase the amount of food grown locally. The countries are unable to grow enough food to feed the population and so they have to rely on imported food.

▲ In addition to farming dairy cattle, some farms also rear camels for their milk.

Fishing is an important part of the economy today. It is mostly **artisanal**, which means it is carried out by small businesses often using traditional techniques. A newer idea in the region is fish farming, where an area of the sea is enclosed and a particular type of fish is raised.

▲ Governments help people develop modern methods in the fishing industry.

Pearl diving was once a major industry. When cultured pearls were introduced by Japan in the 1940s, the pearl-diving industry ended. Some companies are now raising cultured pearls in the waters of the Arabian Gulf.

Other industries in the primary sector are called **extraction industries** because they extract (take out) resources from the ground. These industries include oil and gas drilling, mining and quarrying.

Rocks and minerals come from mines and quarries. Mining and quarrying have negative effects on the environment. They spoil the natural landscape, produce huge amounts of waste and can also create pollution. Serious environmental problems arise from the oil industry if there are major leaks or spills.

Mining and quarrying industries are found in the mountainous areas of the UAE, Oman and Saudi Arabia. Drilling for oil and gas occurs both **offshore** and on land.

▲ Countries around the Arabian Gulf have access to huge amounts of oil and gas.

Activities

1 Work in a group to make a list of materials produced by the primary sector.

2 Make a labelled drawing of one item from your list for a display.

4.14 The economy 2

The secondary sector

The secondary sector of an economy includes all the businesses that use the raw materials provided by the primary sector. Processing industries make changes to a raw material or create new materials. Manufacturing industries make new items, usually by putting separate parts together.

Major processing industries in the countries of the Arabian Gulf include oil refining and **gas liquefaction**. Other important industrial processes include the production of aluminium and steel.

Processing industries in the region also include those involved in making:

- food and drink products
- cement
- soaps and cleaners
- wood products for construction
- paints, solvents, varnishes
- paper
- plastics
- fertilisers.

◀ Modern homes have many items from the processing industries.

Manufacturing industries create the physical things that people need.

New materials created in the processing industries help manufacturing industries to develop. A good example is in shipbuilding. The traditional wooden dhow has been made for hundreds of years and is still made by some craftsmen today.

Many modern shipbuilders now make boats from steel, aluminium or **fibreglass**. Major cities in Arabian Gulf countries have areas where many processing and manufacturing industries are located.

▲ The traditional techniques from the long heritage of shipbuilding are still used today.

The tertiary sector

The tertiary sector is sometimes called the 'service sector' because it provides services rather than goods. The service may be for an individual, for example as a personal trainer, or for a business, for example a delivery service.

People are willing to pay for these services because they do not have the time or the skills necessary to do the things themselves.

The tertiary sector is important because it provides services that people simply want, such as entertainment, and also provides services, such as transportation or communication, that allow other businesses to keep operating.

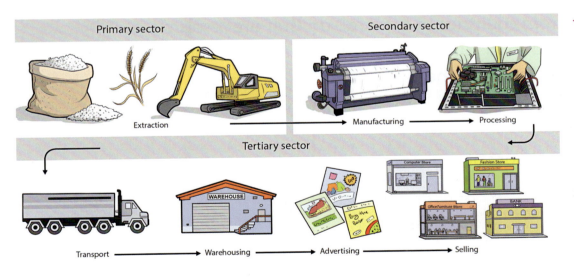

◀ The different sectors of the economy depend on each other.

Activities

1 Work in a group to make a list of materials and products provided by the secondary sector.

2 Make a labelled drawing of one item from your list for a display.

4.15 Service industries

> **In this lesson you will learn:**
> - about some important industries in the tertiary sector.

Trade

Trade, sometimes called **commerce**, is to do with the buying and selling of goods and services. **Domestic trade** takes place within the borders of a country. This means that goods and services are both made or provided and sold within that country. Part of domestic trade is made up of **wholesalers**. Wholesalers buy goods in large quantities. They sell these on to **retailers** who buy smaller amounts. Retailers then sell the goods to individual customers.

International trade involves trading goods between countries. Goods that a country sells outside its borders are called **exports**. Goods that a country buys from other countries are called **imports**.

Major exports from countries of the Arabian Gulf are resources such as oil and gas and foods such as dates and dried fish. Major imports include cars, **textiles**, machinery and food.

Transport

Transport is a vital part of the economy.

◀ Primary industries use transport to move the resources they produce to where they are needed.

Domestic trade uses trucks and vans of different sizes to move goods between ports, warehouses and retailers.

International trade makes use of large ships, aeroplanes and trucks to move goods. The ships can carry large amounts of goods at one time. Aeroplanes carry less but are much faster and so they are used for goods that do not keep so well such as fruits, vegetables and cut flowers. These products pass through our region from places like India on their way to markets in Europe or the United States.

Public transport moves people to and from work and to places for shopping or leisure.

Finance

Finance is to do with how money is used and handled. Almost everyone has some dealings with part of the financial sector.

Banks are institutions that will lend people and businesses money. People may need to borrow money to make a large purchase. Businesses might need to buy or rent new equipment or new premises.

People and businesses also use banks to keep safe the money they have made. They may also choose to **invest** some money in other people's businesses.

Communication

The economy relies on communication. In trade, people can order goods and services thousands of miles away from where those things are produced or provided.

A recent development has been **e-commerce**. This is the name given to trading over the internet.

▲ Customers do not have to travel to a physical location but can order goods and services on a computer.

Activity

Work in a group to discuss items that can be bought over the internet. Write and draw a picture strip that shows how different parts of the economy are involved in getting those items to customers.

4.16 Work

In this lesson you will learn:
- to identify the different occupations in the economy.

Work in the primary sector

The primary sector provides raw materials. Industries that produce rocks, minerals, oil and gas employ **geologists** who know which rocks are useful and where oil and gas might be found. Others working in these industries are miners, drill operators, **engineers** and safety officers.

The agricultural industry employs people who grow plants and rear animals but also has work for scientists and engineers.

The fishing industry employs fishermen at sea and also fish farmers. Scientists are employed to study fish and their habitats.

▲ Many jobs in the primary sector involve a lot of physical activity.

Work in the secondary sector

Many jobs in the secondary sector are in factories where raw materials provided by the primary sector are turned into new materials or new items.

Scientists are often employed to invent new processes and create new materials.

In manufacturing, many jobs are to do with assembling items. Craftspeople are manufacturers who work on a small scale. The construction industry employs people in a wide range of tasks.

◀ Some of the jobs from the secondary sector.

Work in the tertiary sector

The tertiary sector provides services for other parts of the economy and for members of the population. Jobs in commercial services include designers, bankers, drivers, shopkeepers, tourist guides and hotel and restaurant workers. Jobs in public services include teachers, kindergarten workers, refuse collectors, police officers, social workers, doctors and nurses.

◀ Some workers in the tertiary sector.

Activity

Work in a group and choose a particular area of activity in either the primary, secondary or tertiary sector. Think of all the different jobs that could be done in this area.

4.17 Household spending

> **In this lesson you will learn:**
> - to identify the things people need to buy
> - to know that money can be spent or saved.

There are a number of common areas of **expenditure** for today's households.

A place to live

Having a place to live is one of our most basic needs. People live in houses, villas, flats and apartments. The type of **accommodation** a person needs depends on circumstances. Some people live alone while others are part of a family. The size of a family affects the size of the accommodation.

People can buy a place to live which means they own it or they can rent. When people rent property they pay a regular amount of money to the owners in exchange for being allowed to live there.

Modern homes have **appliances** that help people to live comfortably. These include items such as washing machines and dishwashers, ovens, microwave ovens and air-conditioning systems. All of these require energy such as electricity or gas; a household needs to set aside a certain amount of money to pay for this.

Food

Food is another essential expense. People need to eat food to stay alive but the food should be of good quality and varied if people are to be healthy. People need to work out the money they need to put aside to enable them to buy the food they need.

Clothing

We need clothing to protect us from the weather. Traditional Arab clothing is quite simple and effective. Today there are many more choices because styles of clothing from other parts of the world have become a part of life in Arabian Gulf countries. Many people have far more clothes than they actually need for protection. Clothing has become more to do with how a person looks.

Recreation and self-improvement

Recreation is time spent doing things for enjoyment, away from work. Recreational activities away from home include holidays, days out, entertainment, gyms, clubs, sports clubs and fitness centres. Recreation in the home can involve the use of devices such as televisions, computers and games consoles. People may also take part in courses to learn new skills.

Transport

It is almost impossible to live in a modern country and especially in a modern city without access to some form of transport. People may have their own private transport and in most situations they can make use of public transport.

▲ Public transport links different places within a city.

Saving

People can also save money. They do this to build up a certain amount of money so that they can:

- afford an expensive item
- have money available for an expense that they did not expect
- have money to use later on in their life.

Activity

Work in a group to list all the different things which a typical household has to spend money on. Sort the items into three categories: most important, quite important and added extras.

4.18 Money matters

In this lesson you will learn:
- about having a responsible attitude towards money
- to consider how much money people need to have.

Cash and cards

Money is known as the currency of a country. It is available today as cash, in the form of coins and bank notes, and as credit.

People can use cash to buy items at market stalls and in shops. Today it is also possible to use a debit card or a credit card. A debit card is provided to a customer of a bank or other financial institution. The customer keeps a certain amount of money in an account. When a person uses a debit card in a shop or on the internet, the amount of money involved is taken out of the buyer's account and put into the account of the seller straight away.

People can also pay for goods and services using a credit card. This works in a similar way to a debit card except that the money does not come out of the buyer's account straight away. Instead the money is paid to the seller by the financial institution that issued the card and the buyer has to pay them back at a later date. Sometimes the whole amount of a purchase is paid off after a short period. In other cases people pay off smaller, regular amounts of the debt until the whole amount has been paid.

No matter how people pay for things, learning to manage money is an important part of life for adults and children. Money is an important resource and people have to work hard to earn it. We should try to make sure we use money wisely and do not waste it.

What can we spend our money on?

▲ There is a huge range of things that we can buy.

Money provides for our basic needs but also allows us to enjoy other parts of life and to buy things that will be useful or will give us pleasure. As well as buying things, we can choose to spend money on activities such as trips to the cinema or membership of a sports club.

We can also save some money, spend money on other people or give some to charity.

Activities

1 Make a list of the things on which you spend money or that other people spend on your behalf.

2 Work in a group to discuss your list from Activity 1. Say how you feel about the things that you spend money on or are bought for you and then think about how other people might feel about it.

Unit 4 Review questions

1. Rights that are understood to apply to every person in the world are known as:
   a shared rights
   b human rights
   c common rights
   d ethnic rights

2. A natural environment that is spoilt by such things as litter, exhaust fumes or oil spills, is said to be:
   a purified
   b dirty
   c polluted
   d threatened

3. A campaign by a government to promote healthy eating is an example of:
   a a public information campaign
   b a local law
   c a human right
   d an advertising campaign

4. The foundation document for all the laws in a country is known as
   a a charter
   b a declaration
   c a constitution
   d a guarantee

5. Suggest two threats there may be to your local environment and two ways in which people can help to prevent these threats.

6. Describe three skills people need if they are to be good at communicating with others.

7. Describe three laws you think are in place which are intended to make people safer in one way or another.

8. Briefly describe the three main sectors of a country's economy.

9. Give two examples of jobs that can be done in each of the three main sectors of a country's economy.

5 Health and wellbeing

In this unit you will learn:
- the types of food needed in a healthy diet
- how to be healthy and happy, and how to help make a happy society
- how to stay safe on the internet
- to keep a diary of daily activities.

? What do you think people need to be happy?

tooth decay
evaluation
aerobic
rejuvenate
legumes
clot

101

5.1 Good food 1

In these lessons you will learn:
- the importance of eating a balanced diet
- about the different food groups in a healthy diet
- how the body uses the nutrients from the different foods
- how people can be encouraged to eat a healthy diet.

To be healthy we need to drink enough water, make sure we exercise and get enough rest and sleep. We also need to eat a balanced diet that gives our body all the different things it needs. We should eat the right amount of food from each of the four main food groups; carbohydrates, proteins, fats and vitamins and minerals.

> **Did you know?**
> Energy is measured in calories. There are 4 calories in a gram of sugar and 1 calorie in a gram of rice.

Carbohydrates

Carbohydrates give you energy. Your body uses more energy when you are really active but you still use energy when you are not moving and even when you are sleeping. Your body uses energy to pump blood around and to keep itself at the right temperature. It takes energy for your body to grow and to repair itself or recover from an illness.

Simple carbohydrates are sugars and they provide energy to the body very quickly. Sugars are found naturally in fruits and dairy products such as milk. These foods have other nutrients which are good for the body. Sugars are also in things like sweets and fizzy drinks which do not contain other things that are useful for the body. Eating sweets or drinking sugary drinks regularly may lead to **tooth decay**.

Complex carbohydrates provide energy more slowly. They are found in starchy foods made from grains such as bread, pasta and cereal and from some vegetables such as potatoes and sweetcorn.

We have to balance the amount of energy we get from the food we eat with the amount we use up. If there is too little input of energy compared to the output of energy we use then we will feel tired and unable to do very much. Over a period of time the body will lose weight. If the input of energy is greater than the amount we use up then it can be stored as fat and the body may put on weight.

▲ Complex carbohydrates release energy slowly so that the body can keep going for longer periods.

◀ We use a lot of energy when we are very active and need to replace it by eating more food.

Proteins

Proteins build muscles and organs and help your body to repair itself. They come from foods like fish, meat, nuts, **legumes**, eggs, milk and cheese.

Fats

Fats provide a reserve of energy and create a layer to protect some vital organs. Fats help to keep the skin and hair healthy. Some of the vitamins we need are moved around the body in fat.

5.2 Good food 2

Vitamins

Each vitamin performs a special function:

- Vitamin D is good for growing and keeping healthy bones and teeth. Vitamin D is found in oily fish and eggs.

- Vitamin C helps your body to heal if it has a cut and keeps hair, gums and body cells healthy. Good sources of vitamin C are oranges, red and green peppers, broccoli and potatoes.

- Vitamin A helps your body fight off infections and keeps skin healthy. It also helps you to see in dim light. Good sources of vitamin A are cheese, eggs, sweet potatoes, carrots and yoghurt.

- Vitamin E protects cells and tissues from damage and helps to keep blood healthy. Foods with vitamin E include leafy green vegetables, vegetable oils, nuts and egg yolks.

- Vitamin K helps blood to **clot**. Vitamin K is in leafy green vegetables and dairy products.

- B vitamins are a group of vitamins that do many jobs. They help to make the energy in your body and release it when it is needed.

▲ We need to eat a mixture of foods to make sure we get the vitamins and minerals we need.

The vitamins we need are either fat soluble or water soluble. Vitamins that are fat soluble include A, D, E and K. When we eat foods that have these vitamins in them, the vitamins stay in the fat tissues of our body and in our liver. Fat soluble vitamins can stay in the body for a long time until the body needs to use them. Water soluble vitamins are C and a large group of B vitamins. These vitamins do not last so long and so they need to be replaced more often, by eating the foods that contain them.

Minerals

Calcium helps to build strong teeth and bones, to regulate muscle contractions, including the heartbeat, and helps with blood clotting. Good sources of calcium include milk, broccoli, cabbage, nuts and soya beans.

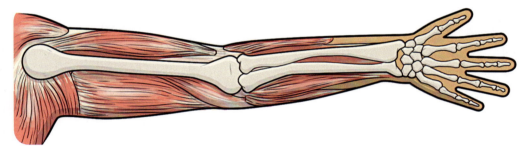

▲ Strong bones are important because our skeleton supports our body and protects vital organs.

Iron has many important roles for the body but is perhaps most important because it makes red blood cells which carry oxygen around the body. We get iron from eating meat, beans, nuts, dried fruit, wholegrain cereals and dark green leafy vegetables.

Other minerals the body uses are potassium and zinc.

Activities

1. Carry out a survey of how food is displayed in shops and how it is advertised. Hold a class discussion on how well you think the idea of eating a healthy diet is promoted.
2. Work in a group to think of and plan a campaign that the government could use to promote healthy eating.

5.3 Respiration and circulation

In this lesson you will learn:
- about respiration and circulation
- how exercise helps your respiration and circulation systems.

Respiration and breathing

Plants and animals use oxygen to help turn the nutrients they get into energy. People too use their breathing system to get oxygen into their body.

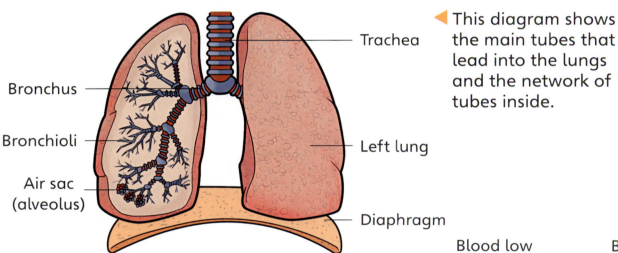

◀ This diagram shows the main tubes that lead into the lungs and the network of tubes inside.

When you inhale (breathe in), your diaphragm is pulled downwards by some strong muscles. As this happens your lungs fill with air and your rib cage expands. Your lungs have a network of very thin tubes, each of which leads to a tiny air sac, called an alveolus. Each air sac is surrounded by narrow tubes, called capillaries which are carrying blood coming from the heart. The tissues making up the air sac are so thin that gases can pass easily between the air sacs and the blood capillaries.

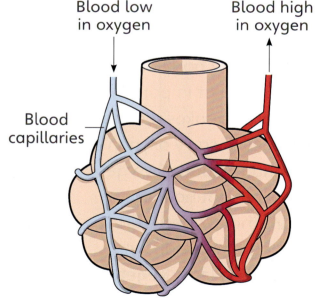

▲ This enlarged view of the air sacs shows how they are surrounded by blood capillaries.

Some of the oxygen in the air you breathe in passes through the tissues of an air sac and enters the blood. The oxygen is taken round the body in the blood. The blood then goes back to the heart to be pumped to all the other parts of your body where the oxygen is used up. Blood, which is now low in oxygen, returns to a different part of the heart, from where it is pumped back to the lungs for the process to start all over again. As the blood (which is low in oxygen) passes around the air sacs, carbon dioxide passes into the air sacs to be sent out of your body when you exhale (breathe out).

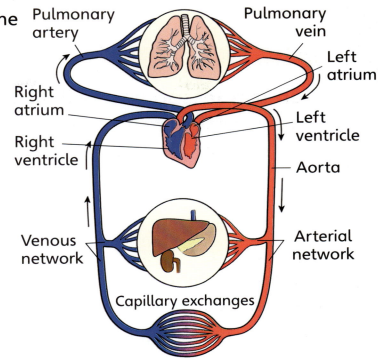

▲ The circulation system.

The benefits of exercise

When you do any **aerobic** exercises, such as running, your body needs more oxygen. The oxygen is being used to help turn nutrients from food and some of your fat stores into energy. Your brain sends signals to your body so that your breathing rate goes up and your heart pumps faster.

The more you do this kind of exercise the more efficient the system becomes. Each breath takes in a greater volume of air than when you are not exercising.

The air exchange rate also improves with exercise. This means that oxygen is more easily taken into the body and carbon dioxide is more readily removed. It is thought that efficient air exchange helps to reduce stress and anxiety and improves physical health and mental wellbeing.

> ## Activity
> Write an explanation, with illustrations, of the benefits of exercise for your circulation system. Say why each person has a responsibility to exercise.

5.4 Happiness

In this lesson you will learn:
- to consider what makes you happy
- to think about what makes other people happy
- why it is important for people to be happy.

Happiness

It is a normal part of human life to want to be happy. We use the word happiness in two different ways.

Firstly, we talk about happiness as an emotion. The emotion makes us feel good and we sometimes express it by smiling or even laughing. If we were asked to explain what was happening we would say we felt happy.

▲ Certain things make us feel happy.

We also talk about happiness as an **evaluation**. This is when we think about how happy we are about a particular situation or event.

If we decide we are unhappy with a situation because we think it could be better, then we can try to make changes to that situation. We hope that we will be more satisfied, or happier, with the improved situation.

When you do a piece of work in school you may be quite happy with it but know that it could be better. Your teacher might look at the work with you and suggest improvements. If you make these improvements, then you will be happier with the end result.

Happiness for everyone

As people we live in groups and our own happiness as individuals is often linked to the happiness of other people. For example, we know that it is not good to be selfish and only think about ourselves and what we want. We should always be aware of the needs and feelings of other people.

It is also possible for us to be unhappy about a situation even if we are not directly involved. When we think about people who are living in very difficult circumstances we know that they are probably unhappy. Many people want to do something to change this situation and so they donate money to charity or volunteer some of their time.

▲ When we learn about people whose lives are very challenging we often want to do things to change the situation for the better.

Activities

1 Work with a friend to discuss how happy you are with life in school. Suggest one idea that you think will improve school life.

2 Work in a group to research some charities working to help people in difficult circumstances in your country or elsewhere in the world.

5.5 What makes people happy?

In this lesson you will learn:
- to identify what makes people happy
- to consider what creates a happy society.

Feeling safe, secure and loved

Feelings of safety, security and of being loved are the foundations of happiness for most people. The family is the place where we should experience these more than anywhere else. That is partly why the family is such an important unit in society. Other close social groups such as friends also have an important effect on our sense of belonging and happiness.

Stress and anxiety

People's happiness is also affected by the levels of stress and anxiety they feel. People can feel these on a personal level, for example if they are taking a test or facing a particular challenge. The level of stress and anxiety felt by people in a country is affected by how safe and peaceful they feel the country to be.

Money

Money allows people to provide the things they need to survive. People who are very poor are less able to do this and so are more likely to feel unhappy or dissatisfied with their lives.

If people have more than enough money to provide for all their basic needs, then they can spend money on making their life more comfortable or enjoyable.

▲ There is a lot of debate about how much happier being wealthy actually makes people feel.

Justice and fairness

If people feel that a situation is unfair or unjust, then they are likely to be less happy with it. They may feel they have been treated unfairly but can also be unhappy to see others being treated in this way. It is also hard to be truly happy with a situation if that happiness has come about because of circumstances that make someone else less happy.

A good life

Since ancient times, many people have believed that a person could only find happiness by living the right kind of life. This often meant that people should not focus on material things for themselves but should instead think about their relationships and the needs of other people. People have also thought that people who try their best at whatever they are doing and work hard to achieve their goals are more likely to be happy.

◀ Having a caring attitude to the natural world is also thought to promote happiness.

Activity

Think about the ideas on these pages and write about your level of happiness and how it could be changed. Write about a goal you have faced or will face in the future. Say what you did or are doing to achieve your goal.

5.6 Rest and relaxation

In this lesson you will learn:
- to understand the importance of rest and relaxation
- about leisure time
- to identify positive uses of leisure time.

The importance of rest and relaxation

Rest and relaxation are important parts of a healthy lifestyle for people of every age. Resting helps your body to **rejuvenate** and allows your mind to stay clear. Rest helps you to avoid extremes of mood and helps with learning, understanding and remembering. Too little rest means that all these things suffer and your body is also less able to fight off infections and disease.

Relaxation is to do with removing tension and stress. People often feel pressures from their work or study and it is important that those pressures do not stop them from finding the time to relax.

Relaxing the body is helped by gentle stretching and by tensing and then relaxing muscles. Sleeping is obviously a time when the body can relax but simply resting from activity also helps the body to recover. Relaxing is also about resting the mind. We often have things that cause us to be worried or to feel anxious. If we clear our mind of those thoughts for a short time it can reduce the level of stress we feel. It is also often the case that we come back to the situation and are able to think about it more clearly.

Time alone

Spending just a short time alone in a quiet place is a good way of relaxing. Time spent like this allows you to think carefully about how you are feeling. It helps you decide if there are any changes you would like to make about the things that concern you.

At other times you might choose to do something that you enjoy such as painting or reading. For relaxation you need to choose something that is not too stimulating or exciting.

◀ Some activities are naturally relaxing.

Leisure time

Our leisure time is the time when we are not working, studying, looking after ourselves or completing household chores. Leisure time makes it possible for us to join clubs or take classes to learn new skills. It is also when we can spend time with our family and friends. These times are important because they help us to create and build strong personal relationships.

▲ There are many positive ways to spend our leisure time.

Activities

1. Write about the things you enjoy doing that help you to relax.
2. Keep a diary of all your activities, including times when you relax.

5.7 Be safe on the internet 1

In these lessons you will learn:
- about the need to be safe on the internet
- to identify safe practices when using the internet
- to know what personal information is and what to share.

The internet

The internet is a system linking computers and other devices all over the world. The World Wide Web is a way of communicating and sharing information and knowledge around the internet. The internet is sometimes referred to as a 'virtual world', 'the digital world' and as 'cyberspace' but it has important effects in the real world.

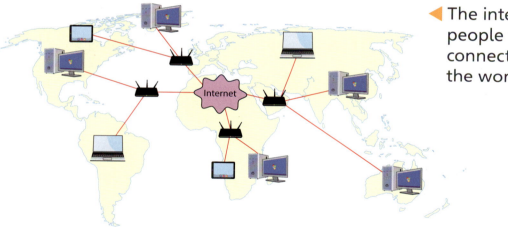

◀ The internet allows people to make connections around the world.

Behaviour on the internet

The rules for behaviour in the digital environment of the internet are the same as anywhere else.

When using the internet people should behave with consideration and respect, remembering that what happens 'online' can have an impact on other parts of life.

Your identity

You have a unique identity. You can decide how much another person gets to find out about you in real life. The same is true on the internet.

The more information you provide such as photos or interests, helps people identify you.

Personal information

Your personal information includes things such as your name, age, address, home phone number, your mobile phone number and your school. Other personal information includes your hobbies and interests, places you go, such as sports clubs, things you do and even how you feel.

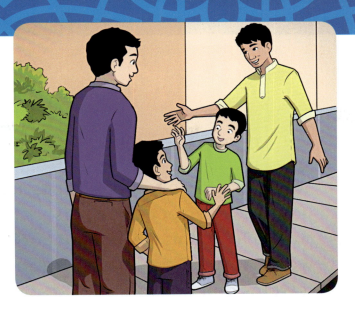

▲ When people meet face to face they can identify one another. Each one knows who the other person is.

Personal information and the internet

We are happy to communicate freely over the internet with friends and family. Social media sites are based on people sharing their personal information. However, many other websites also ask people for personal information. It is good to be cautious about sharing personal information when it is not clear who will be able to read it.

▲ Mobile phones are part of the digital world.

Activities

1 Make a list of guidelines that tell people how they should behave in the 'digital world'.

2 Work in a group to discuss the type of information you would be happy to share on the internet and the information that you would keep private.

5.8 Be safe on the internet 2

Personal responsibility

We have certain responsibilities in life to ourselves and to other people. We accept some personal responsibility for our own safety. To do this we learn about dangers and then behave in a way that keeps our risks to a minimum. We behave with respect towards other people and do not do or say things that would hurt them or put them in danger. All of this applies when we are using the internet just as much as in the physical world.

Internet identity

When you use some sites on the internet you can create a **profile**. You do not have to give real information about yourself and can make up a nickname or a user name. This protects your real identity. If everybody else is also protecting their real identity you never really know who the other people on a website are.

◀ We learn about the dangers in the real world and need to do the same for the internet.

Privacy

Many sites allow you to adjust 'privacy settings'. This is a way of limiting the people who will be able to see the information you put on the website. It is sensible to set this to the level where only your friends and family can see it.

It is always sensible to think that whatever you put on the internet could possibly become public. Thinking in this way means you are really careful about what you post.

Passwords

A password limits access to a computer, computer programs, files or profiles. It is a series of letters and numbers that needs to be kept secret. The only other people who should know your password at home are your parents, and in school, your teacher. It is a good idea not even to let friends know your passwords.

Using websites safely

There are a number of ways to decide how good we think a website is. For example, if we are looking for information we need to be sure that it is reliable and up to date. We need to be able to read the material and find our way round the site easily.

Whatever type of site we are using we must be aware of other content that may appear, such as adverts and links. These can sometimes take us to unknown sites or even download viruses. We should always talk to an adult before we decide to use an unknown website or download new content.

Activity

Work in a group to create a set of guidelines to help people choose appropriate websites.

Unit 5 Review questions

1. Sugars are simple carbohydrates that provide:
   a. energy slowly to help your body keep moving for long periods
   b. vitamins to help maintain a healthy skin
   c. protein to build muscles
   d. energy quickly and for a short period

2. Calcium is an example of a group of nutrients called:
   a. vitamins
   b. minerals
   c. fats
   d. sugars

3. The process of breathing in and breathing out is known as:
   a. circulation
   b. irrigation
   c. respiration
   d. perspiration

4. During aerobic exercise your body needs:
   a. more oxygen
   b. less oxygen
   c. less energy
   d. more carbon dioxide

5. Explain why people need to eat a balanced and varied diet, giving at least two examples of certain food groups and how the body uses them.

6. Describe a meal that you think contains a good balance of healthy foods.

7. Briefly explain the benefits of regular exercise to an individual.

8. Explain why people have a responsibility to exercise and eat well in order to maintain their own health.

9. Explain why it is important for people to have rest and relaxation and describe two ways in which you get these things for yourself.

10. Write some brief guidelines for people who are new users of the internet about how they can protect themselves.

Glossary

accommodation a place to live and work

aerobic exercises designed to improve respiration and circulation, for example running

agriculture the practice of farming to grow crops or to rear animals

appliance items such as washing machines or microwaves that help people to live more comfortably

aquifer an area of rock which is able to contain water underground

artisanal a business that is carried out on a small scale, such as fishing by local fishermen

axis on a graph or chart, a fixed line against which the positions of points are measured

bauxite soft mineral used to make aluminium

BCE an abbreviation for 'Before the Common Era', part of a year-numbering system which uses the beginning of the life of Jesus Christ as a reference point. BCE applies to all the years before this point

billboard a large board on the outside of a building or at the side of a road used for advertising

borders lines marking the limits of the area covered by a country, as shown on maps

caliph a religious and political leader in early Islam

caliphate the state ruled by a caliph

capital city the place where the government of a country is located. Capital cities usually have the largest population in a country

caravan a group of people travelling together, possibly as traders or pilgrims, sometimes using camels or pack animals

CE an abbreviation for 'Common Era', part of a year-numbering system which uses the beginning of the life of Jesus Christ as a reference point. The Common Era begins from this point

charcoal a fuel made by burning wood slowly in an oven with little air

city state a large town and all its surrounding territory, under the control of a single ruler or group

civilisation a culture that has become quite complex and has developed areas such as the arts, maths and science

clot to thicken and become solid

cohesion the act of being united, often used when talking about groups of people in a community or society

commerce the activity of buying and selling, especially on a large scale

commodities items that can be traded, for example in historical times incense, spices, silk

compass rose a design on a map showing compass directions

constitution a legal document laying down all principles and ideas that guide other laws within a country

cosmetics beauty products, such as lipstick

council a group of people who meet to discuss issues and make decisions about action that should be taken

current affairs events in government or in society that are happening at the present time and are often discussed in the media

customs an accepted way of behaving or doing things in a culture or society

democracy a system where the government is elected by the people of a country

desalination the process of removing salt from sea water

digital signboard electronic notices often used in busy public places such as airports where information needs to be updated

domestic trade exchange of goods within the borders of a particular country

e-commerce trading carried out on the internet

embroidered decorated with beautiful and often complicated sewn patterns

engineer a person whose job is to design and build machines, engines, roads or bridges

evaluation a reasoned judgment about the quality of something

evaporate to turn from liquid into a gas

expenditure an amount of money spent

exports goods sold from one country to another

extraction industries the industries involved in taking materials out of the Earth

fertilisers substances added to soil to make plants grow more successfully

fibreglass a strong, light material made from glass fibres and plastic, used for making boats, etc

gas liquefaction the process of turning a gas into a liquid

gem a precious or semi-precious stone

geologist a scientist who studies the Earth, including the origin and history of the rocks and soil of which the Earth is made

goods physical items produced by human activity to meet people's needs

governorate administrative division of a country ruled by a governor

grazing a description of animals that eat grass and other plants in an area of land

groundwater water stored beneath the Earth's surface in the spaces within soil and rock

guarantee a promise that certain things will happen

gypsum a soft grey mineral used in fertilisers and in the building industry

habitat the place where a particular type of plant or animal is found

heritage the traditions, beliefs and achievements that are in the history of a people or country

immunisation protection from a disease, especially by giving an injection of a vaccine

imports goods bought by one country from another

independent when countries have their own government

institution an organisation which has a specific purpose such as education or the law

international trade exchange of goods between one country and another

interpersonal related to relationships between people

interval in graphs or charts, the space between two points on an axis

invest to put money into something, for example a company or business, in the hope of making a profit

key a table explaining the symbols used on a map

legumes plants with seeds in long pods, for example peas, beans

livestock animals raised in an agricultural setting to produce meat or other products

marginal on the edge or 'in the margin' of a map or a page

marine related to the sea

medicinal a substance that has properties which are helpful to treat illness or infection

migrate to move permanently from one place to another

ministry a department within government that looks after a particular area, such as health or education

monarchy in a monarchy a single person, the monarch, has ultimate power

motto a short phrase that sums up the ideas or principles of an organisation or country

municipal authority a government body with certain powers within a town or municipal area

municipality a town or city with its own local government

nomadic communities who move from place to place with their animals

non-renewable resources that can be used only once, for example gas or coal

offshore situated at sea

policies a plan of action agreed or chosen by a government

population the total number of people living in an area

post to put information or other material on a website

precipitation the different forms in which water falls to the ground from the sky. Water can fall as rain, snow or hail

principles a rule or belief that helps to identify what is right or wrong and that guides actions and behaviour

profile on a computer, a visual display of personal information

public sector part of the economy controlled and operated by the state

raw materials basic materials from which others are made

rejuvenate to become full of energy

relief (on a map) the use of colours and lines to show heights of hills, valleys, etc

republic a system in which people elected by citizens of a country have authority to rule

retailer a trader who buys quantities of goods from a supplier and sells smaller quantities on to customers, usually in a store or supermarket

sanitation the process of keeping places and people clean and free from dirt and infection through good hygiene and the removal of waste

scale on a map, scale refers to the relationship between a measurement on the map and a measurement in real life on the surface of the Earth

sector an area of the economy where industries are involved in a particular range of activities

services in the economy, services involve doing something for customers but not producing goods

sharia law the legal system of Islam

sightseeing visiting places of interest

Society people living together in an organised community who share traditions, values and laws

statistics information such as data or facts shown in the form of numbers

sustainability using natural resources in a way that does not harm the environment

technology machinery and other devices developed for helping in human activities

terrain the physical features over an area of land

textiles cloth or woven fabric

tooth decay damage to the teeth caused by poor hygiene or diet

tourists people travelling and visiting places for pleasure

traditions customs and beliefs developed by a society and handed down through different generations

transactions business agreements between people for the exchange of goods and services

urban relating to a town or city

values the things in life that people think are important, for example kindness, honesty, respect

vulnerable weak and easily hurt physically or emotionally

water table the level at and below which water is found in the ground

welfare a person's health, happiness and safety

wholesalers traders who buy very large quantities of goods, from manufacturers or suppliers of raw materials including foods

Great Clarendon Street, Oxford, OX2 6DP, United Kingdom

Oxford University Press is a department of the University of Oxford. It furthers the University's objective of excellence in research, scholarship, and education by publishing worldwide. Oxford is a registered trade mark of Oxford University Press in the UK and in certain other countries

© Pat Lunt 2015

The moral rights of the author have been asserted

First published in 2015

All rights reserved. No part of this publication may be reproduced, stored in a retrieval system, or transmitted, in any form or by any means, without the prior permission in writing of Oxford University Press, or as expressly permitted by law, by licence or under terms agreed with the appropriate reprographics rights organization. Enquiries concerning reproduction outside the scope of the above should be sent to the Rights Department, Oxford University Press, at the address above.

You must not circulate this work in any other form and you must impose this same condition on any acquirer

British Library Cataloguing in Publication Data
Data available

9780198356844

10 9 8 7

Paper used in the production of this book is a natural, recyclable product made from wood grown in sustainable forests. The manufacturing process conforms to the environmental regulations of the country of origin.

Printed by Repro India Ltd.

Acknowledgements

The publishers would like to thank the following for permissions to use their photographs:

Cover photo: Richard Nowitz/National Geographic/Offset, P3: Jochen Tack/imageBROKER/Corbis/Image Library, P9: Bryn Lennon/Getty Images, P14: Philip Lange/Shutterstock, P15: Mariia Savoskula/Shutterstock, P17a: ANADOLU AGENCY/Getty Images, P17b: Kami/arabianEye/Corbis/ Image Library, P18: Grapeheast/Getty Images, P21: Adam Woolfitt/Corbis/Image Library, P23: Cui Xinyu/Xinhua Press/Corbis/Image Library, P25: The Art Archive / Alamy, P27a: Shutterstock.com, P27b: Robert Harding Picture Library Ltd / Alamy Stock Photo, P31: Sofiaworld/Shutterstock, P33a: Gianni Dagli Orti/Corbis/Image Library, P33b: Angelo Hornak/ Alamy Stock Photo, P35a: JOHN KELLERMAN / Alamy Stock Photo, P35b: Ursula Gahwiler/Robert Harding/Getty Images, P37: shutterstock.com, P46: Frans Lemmens/Corbis/Image Library, P49: Reza/National Geographic/Getty Images, P50: Byelikova Oksana/shutterstock, P51: ANADOLU AGENCY/Getty Images, P52: Xinhua/Xinhua Press/Corbis/Image Library, P53a: Richard Allenby-Pratt/ArabianEye/Getty Images, P53b: Henglein and Steets/Cultura/Corbis/Image Library, P56: Ogaman/shutterstock, P57: Danita Delimont/Gallo Images/Getty Images, P61: Shutterstock.com, P63: Philip Lange / Shutterstock.com, P64: Stas Moroz/shutterstock, P65: Mahmoud illean/Demotix/Corbis/Image Library, P67: VStock LLC/Tetra Images/Corbis/Image Library, P68: Grapheast /Alamy, P71a: Travel Ink/Gallo Images/Getty Images, P71b: SEUX Paule/hemis.fr/Getty Images, P72: JonMilnes/Shutterstock, P73a: S-F / Shutterstock.com, P73b: Lason Athanasiadis/Corbis/Image Library, P75: ImageBROKER/Alamy, P76:   Kevin Dodge/Corbis/Image Library, P78: Celia Peterson/arabianEye/Corbis/Image Library, P79: Crackshots/Corbis/Image Library, P81: Art Directors & TRIP/Alamy, P84: Sergio Pitamitz/Corbis/Image Library, P85: Jaxpix / Alamy Stock Photo, P87: Philip Lange/Shutterstock, P88: Kamran Jebreili/AP Photo, P89a: StockStudio / Shutterstock.com, P89b: Barry Iverson/Alamy, P91: Martin Siepmann/Westend61/Corbis/Image Library, P92: Ugurhan Betin/Photographer's Choice RF/Getty Images, P93: Daryl Visscher/arabianEye/Corbis/Image Library, P97: Philip Lange / Shutterstock.com, P101: Chris Schmidt/+E/Gettyimages, P109: Hikrcn / Shutterstock.com, P111: Ochen Tack/arabianEye/Getty Images, P115: Image Source/Corbis/Image Library, P116: shutterstock.com

Illustrations by Six Red Marbles

Although we have made every effort to trace and contact all copyright holders before publication this has not been possible in all cases. If notified, the publisher will rectify any errors or omissions at the earliest opportunity.

Links to third party websites are provided by Oxford in good faith and for information only. Oxford disclaims any responsibility for the materials contained in any third party website referenced in this work.